MW01068765

Bless the Bees:
The Pending Extinction of our Pollinators and
What You Can Do to Stop It

BY KENNETH EADE

PHOTOGRAPHS BY VALENTINA EADE

TABLE OF CONTENTS

"If the bee disappears from the earth, man would have no more than four years to live." - Albert Einstein.

CHAPTER 1: TO BEE OR NOT TO BE

What Einstein meant is that the bees are an indicator species. Their loss could signal that we are facing a "mass extinction," something biologists fear may be upon us now. If they are right, this would be the sixth mass extinction in world history, the last one being the dinosaurs, and, instead of a meteor hitting the earth, which is suspected to be the cause of their demise, we (mankind) are the cause of it this time.

The bees have survived over 100 million years of evolution, but it has taken us less than 30 years to kill almost all of them off. Bees are responsible for pollinating 60% of the world's food supply and 90% of all flowering plants. Without them, the human race would face starvation. One of every three bites of food comes from plants pollinated by honeybees and other pollinators. Without bees to pollinate our food we would have a worldwide food and economic epidemic. It has been called the *bee apocalypse* by Russia's president, but it is worse in the United States than any other country. Since 1972, feral honey bees in the United States have declined 80% to near extinction, and domestic bees in the United States are down to 60%. Since 2006, the epidemic among honey bees has been referred to as colony collapse disorder (CCD), describing the disappearance of entire colonies of bees. Many native pollinators, such as native bees, bats, birds, wasps and flies, also face extinction due to habitat destruction, climate change, lack of biodiversity and the use of pesticides.

Among the causes cited for this disaster of epidemic proportions are parasites, the decrease in abundance and diversity of wildflowers, insecticides and genetically engineered foods (GMOs) that create their own synthetic pesticides which kill bees as well as other insects, and have been shown to be harmful to humans as well. But one thing is for certain-- mankind is responsible for the drastic decline in bee population and the United States government is doing nothing about it. On the contrary, the government has taken measures to make the problem worse.

Pollination, whereby pollen grains are transferred in the reproduction and fertilization of plants, is an irreplaceable step in the reproduction of seed plants. Most plant fruits are unable to develop without pollination taking place and many beautiful flower varieties would die out if not pollinated. Evolution has produced a symbiotic relationship between the pollinators in the animal world and the plant world. Only 10% of flowering plants are pollinated without their assistance. Imagine never again seeing a flower?

As such, pollinators are a critical link in our food system. More than 85 percent of earth's plant species – many of which compose some of the most nutritional parts of our diet – require pollinators to exist. They are critical components of our environment and essential to our food security. Bees provide the indispensable and free service of pollination to more than 85% of flowering plants, contributing to 60%

of global food production. In the United States alone, 100 crop species rely upon bee pollination to some degree, making up 1/3 of the American food supply, and valued in the billions of dollars to American Agriculture. That's one of every three bites of your food, at every meal, every day.

There is far more to this 100 million year old evolution of pollination than just honey bees, who were not native to the United States, but imported from Europe and probably originally came from Africa. At least 4,000 species of native bees are known to exist in North America alone. Bats, butterflies, moths, birds, wasps and some flies also pollinate plant life. All of them are at risk, and this book will show you how you can make a difference in saving them, our food supply, and our planet as we know it.

What foods would we be missing without our pollinators? Whole Foods Market recently demonstrated this by removing those items from their stores so you could see how limited our selection would be. Not only would we have to exist on products made almost entirely from soy, rice, corn and wheat, which would cause a great nutritional imbalance in our systems, we would also miss the taste of so many wonderful foods that we now take for granted.

Imagine the breakfast table without coffee. Imagine a hot fudge sundae without the chocolate. These foods include" acerola, alfalfa, allspice, almonds, clover, apples, avocado, beets, blackberries, broccoli, brussels sprouts, bukwehat, cabbage, cactus, cantaloupe, melons, caraway, carrots, cauliflower, cashews, celery, chestnuts, chili peppers, bell peppers, green peppers, red peppers, Chinese cabbage, cocoa, coffea arabica, coriander, cranberries, cucumbers, eggplant, elderberry, fennel, figs, flax, grapes, hazel nuts, kiwi, lemons, limes, lima beans, kidney beans, mango, string beans, haricot beans, green beans, loquat, lupine, lychee, macadamia nuts, mango, mustard, naranjillo, oil palm, okra, onions, papaya, peaches, passion fruit, nectarines, pears, persimmon, peas, pomegranate, rapeseed, raspberry, safflower, sesame, cherries, strawberries, sunflowers, tomatoes, tangelo, vanilla, walnut, and watermelon.

CHAPTER 2: THE EUROPEAN HONEY BEE

The Western honey bee, also known as the European honey bee (*apis mellifera*,) although facing extinction, has no legal protection under the U.S. Endangered Species Act or any state endangered species statutes. Human association with the European honey bee spans at least 7,000 years. This species of bee, probably the most familiar to man, is almost entirely domesticated and is not only used to produce hive products, such as honey, wax and royal jelly, but it is also the primary species used for the pollination of agricultural crops globally. *Apis mellifera* initially evolved in Africa and then, in at least two separate events predating the arrival of *Homo sapiens*, migrated north to central Asia and northern Europe, diverging into at least two-dozen distinct sub-species. Domestication, however, has eroded sub-species distinctions through hybridization, particularly in regions such as North America where *Apis mellifera* was not native.

The best evidence of specific pollinator decline can be seen in the honey bee, which is the primary commercial pollinator of agricultural crops in North America and the most widely used, actively managed pollinator in the world. This is because there is more data on losses known to beekeepers than losses that occur in the wild. Data on feral bees is not as available as domesticated bees involved in commercial apiculture.

Honey bees in North America were brought to the New World from Europe in the 1600's. There are 28 subspecies of *apis mellifera*; the most common of which in America is *Apis mellifera lingustica*, the Italian bee.

Honey bees are the best example of a perfect social animal. They live in colonies and all work for the common good of the colony. The Queen, which can live for up to five to six years, is the mother of all the new members of the colony. There is only one queen in each hive, but new queens are generated by the worker bees from queen cells, and are fed a special diet of royal jelly. When a queen is generated, she goes on one mating flight, wherein she can mate with up to 20 male (drone) bees, and stores enough sperm in her body to supply eggs for the hive throughout her life. Drone bees' sole function is to mate with the queen, and, if they are successful, they die afterwards. Worker bees comprise most of the population in the hive. They produce honey and royal jelly, tend to the new bee larvae and the queen, and feed the drones. If the population gets too large in the hive, the worker bees decide when it is time to split the colony. This process, called swarming, is when the old queen flies away with a quantity of bees to establish a new hive. The new queen is left with the old hive.

In the beginning of a worker bee's life, she spends her first days cleaning out brood cells, preparing them for eggs, then nurses the new larva. She then goes into a phase of life where she produces wax, used to make and repair cells. Then workers may attend the queen, ventilate or gather water for the hive, and remove dead bees. Toward the end of a worker bee's life, they go out into the wild to forage for nectar and pollen. They have special places (bags) on their legs for collecting pollen called *corbicuola*. A worker bee in this last cycle of life will keep making trips to flowers and back to the hive until she simply dies in the field. Bees communicate the distance and location of available foraging areas to other bees by "dancing" in a circular motion. They are also known to have the power of human facial recognition. Worker bees can sting, but they die soon thereafter, so they only do so to defend the hive and anything they conceive as a threat. If they come near you, just don't aggress them and you should be fine. Batting at any bee is not a good idea. Just stay still and calm until the bee flies away.

Honey bees have two stomachs, one for digestion and one to store nectar called a *crop*. When the foraging worker bee comes back from a trip, she regurgitates the nectar to a processor worker bee's crop, and heads back out on another foraging trip. The processor regurgitates the nectar into a honeycomb cell where it ripens. As she does this, it adds an enzyme called *invertase*, which breaks the sucrose in the nectar down into glucose and fructose. Complex chemical reactions between the two sugars make honey, a substance which is nutritional, and resistant to mold, bacteria, fungi and microbes. When the nectar has ripened into honey, it has lost most of its water content, and the processor bee caps the honey cell to keep it dry and clean. The honey is used to feed the colony all year long.

Although honey bees are considered domesticated, they do forage in the wild, which makes them susceptible to unknown dangers that humankind has placed in the ecosphere. In fact, if left to their own, honey bees would do quite nicely in the wild. Honey bees have been dying off in large numbers around the world since the mid-1990s. First in France, then in the U.S. and elsewhere, colonies have been mysteriously collapsing with adult bees disappearing, seemingly abandoning their hives. In 2006, about two years after this phenomenon hit the U.S., it was named "Colony Collapse Disorder," or CCD. Each year since commercial beekeepers have reported annual losses of 29% - 36%. Such losses are unprecedented, and more than double what is considered normal.

While wild pollinators like bats and bumble bees are also facing catastrophic declines, managed honey bees are, economically, the most important pollinators in the world. According to a recent U.N. report, of the 100 crops that provide 90% of the world's food, over 70 of them are pollinated by honey bees. In the U.S. alone, honey bees' economic contribution is valued at over $15 billion.

U.S. commercial beekeepers report that their industry is on the verge of collapse, and farmers who rely on pollination services are increasingly concerned. It's unlikely that such a collapse will directly result in a food security crisis, but crop yields would decline significantly, and more acres of land would need to be put into production to meet demand. With most fruits, many vegetables, almonds, alfalfa and many other crops all dependent upon bees for pollination, the variety and nutritional value of our food system is threatened.

In addition to their agricultural value as pollinators, honey bees are a keystone indicator species as to what is going on in our environment. As such, their decline points to, and is likely to accelerate, broader environmental degradation. Pollinator population declines are such an important part of the current collapse in biodiversity that seven in ten biologists believe their demise signals an even greater threat to humanity than the global warming which contributes to the decline. These biologists believe we are in the midst of a sixth mass extinction. To put it into perspective, the last mass extinction the earth knew on such a grand scale was the extinction of the dinosaurs about 65 million years ago.

As an indicator species, honey bees are sounding an alarm that we cannot afford to ignore. Industrial agriculture has gone bezerk, depending on an extremely high use of pesticides that have caused endemic, long lasting effects on the ecosphere. The same manufacturers of these pesticides, such as Monsanto and Bayer in the United States, and Syngenta in Europe, have genetically engineered plant products to be resistant to their pesticides, which has spawned the use of even more pesticides, and they have also genetically engineered crops that produce their own synthetic insecticides, causing a critical imbalance to the environment at the sake of corporate profits. This practice, if left uncontrolled, will result in mono-agricultural crops, such as corn, soy and wheat becoming the exclusive crops in the food supply, thus contributing to malnutrition and the eventual the decline of humans as well. We must stop acting like we are Gods of our own destiny and respect the limits of our mother earth.

CHAPTER 3: COLONY COLLAPSE DISORDER

Colony Collapse Disorder, or "CCD" is a mysterious phenomenon of which no definite cause is known to exist. Its symptoms are the disappearance or death of the entire adult population in hives of honey bees, leaving the brood alone. CCD has reached epidemic proportions in Europe and the United States, leading to a drastic reduction in the current number of active hives. There are many studies which postulate multiple, interacting causes, such as pathogens, climate change, habitat loss, pesticides (including insecticides, fungicides and herbicides) and related immune system and genetic damage over time, that makes the hives defenseless against such parasites as the *varroa* mite, the tracheal mite, and diseases such as foulbrood. Apiculture practices themselves, such as the use of antibiotics, long distance transportation of hives to agriculture pollinating sites, the feeding of high fructose corn syrup as well as exposure to electromagnetic radiation, have also been proposed as contributory causes. Whether any single factor or a combination of factors acting independently are responsible is still unknown. But what is known is that the decline is so rapid that we cannot ignore it and we must ameliorate the practices we know are harmful in order to remediate the decline.

Research in the United States

The primary source of information on CCD is from the Colony Collapse Disorder Working Group, based primarily at Pennsylvania State University. Their preliminary report pointed out some patterns but drew no strong conclusions. A survey of beekeepers early in 2007 indicated that most hobbyist beekeepers believed that starvation was the leading cause of death in their colonies while commercial beekeepers believed that invertebrate pests such as varroa mites, honey bee tracheal mites, and small hive beetles were the leading cause of CCD.

In July 2009, the first annual report of the U.S. Colony Collapse Disorder Steering Committee was published, suggesting that CCD may be caused by the interaction of many agents in combination. Also in 2009, they published a comprehensive descriptive study that concluded: "Of the 61 variables quantified (including adult bee physiology, pathogen loads, and pesticide levels), no single factor was found with enough consistency to suggest one causal agent. Bees in CCD colonies had higher pathogen loads and were co-infected with more pathogens than control populations, suggesting either greater pathogen exposure or reduced defenses in CCD bees."

The second annual Steering Committee report was released in November 2010. The group reported that although many associations, including pesticides, parasites, and pathogens have been identified throughout the course of research, "it is becoming increasingly clear that no single factor alone is responsible for [CCD]". Their findings, however, indicated an absence of damaging levels of the parasite *Nosema* or parasitic Varroa mites at the time of collapse.

The findings included an association of sub-lethal effects of some pesticides with CCD, including two common miticides in particular, *coumaphos* and *fluvalinate*, which are pesticides registered for use by beekeepers to control varroa mites. It was reported that studies also identified sub-lethal effects of neonicotinoids and fungicides. It is thought that these pesticides impair the bee's immune system, which leaves the bee more susceptible to bee viruses.

A 2010 survey of healthy and CCD-affected colonies also revealed elevated levels of pesticides in wax and pollen, but the amounts of pesticides were similar in both failing and healthy hives. They also confirmed suspected links between CCD and poor colony health, inadequate diet, and long-distance transportation. Studies continue to show very high levels of pathogens in CCD-affected samples and lower pathogen levels in non-affected samples, consistent with the empirical observation that healthy honey bee colonies normally fend off pathogens. These observations have led to the hypothesis that bee declines are resulting from immune suppression.

In the March 2012, issue of the journal *Science*, two separate studies found that neonicotinoid insecticides may interfere with bee's natural homing abilities, causing them to become disoriented and preventing them from finding their way back to the hive. This is a major symptom of CCD. The U.S. Department of Agriculture agrees. Scientists have long been concerned that pesticides and possibly some fungicides may have sub-lethal effects on bees, not killing them outright but instead impairing their development and behavior. Of special interest is the class of insecticides called neonicotinoids, which contain the active ingredients *imidacloprid*, and similar other chemicals, such as *clothianidin* and *thiamethoxam*. Honey bees may be affected by such chemicals when they are used as a seed treatment because they are known to work their way through the plant up into the flowers and leave residues of the poison in the nectar and pollen. Scientists note that the doses taken up by bees are not lethal, but they are concerned about possible chronic problems caused by long-term exposure.

Virtually all of the genetically engineered (GMO) Bt corn grown in the U.S. is treated with neonicotinoids and a 2012 study found high levels of clothianidin in pneumatic planter exhaust. In the study, it was found that the insecticide was present in the soil of unplanted fields nearby those planted with Bt corn and also on dandelions (a favorite of bees) growing near those fields.

Research in 2008 by scientists from Pennsylvania State University found high levels of the pesticides *fluvalinate* and *coumaphos* in samples of wax from hives, as well as lower levels of 70 other pesticides. These chemicals have been used to try to eradicate varroa mites. Researchers from Washington State University in 2009 confirmed high levels of pesticide residue in hive wax and found an association between it and significantly reduced bee longevity. The work also focused on the impact of the microsporidian pathogen *Nosema ceranae*, the build-up of which was high in the majority of the bees tested, even after large doses of the antibiotic *fumagillin*.

Research in Europe

In 2012, several peer reviewed independent studies were published showing that neonicotinoids had previously undetected routes of exposure affecting bees, including through dust, pollen, and nectar, and that sub-nanogram toxicity resulted in failure to return to the hive without immediate lethality, which is the primary symptom of CCD. Research also showed environmental persistence of the pesticides in agricultural irrigation channels and soil. These reports prompted a formal peer review by the European Food Safety Authority (EFSA), which stated in January 2013 that some neonicotinoids pose an unacceptably high risk to bees. Their review concluded, "A high acute risk to honey bees was identified from exposure via dust drift for the seed treatment uses in maize (corn,) oilseed rape and cereals. A high acute risk was also identified from exposure via residues in nectar and/or pollen." David Goulson, an author of one of the studies which prompted the EFSA review, has suggested that industry science pertaining to neonicotinoids may have been deliberately deceptive, and the UK Parliament has asked manufacturer Bayer Cropscience to explain discrepancies in evidence they have submitted to an investigation.

A 2010 survey reported 98 pesticides and metabolites detected in aggregate concentrations up to 214 ppm in bee pollen—this figure represents over half of the individual pesticide incidences ever reported for apiaries. It was suggested that "while exposure to many of these neurotoxicants elicits acute and sub lethal reductions in honey bee fitness, the effects of these materials in combinations and their direct association with CCD or declining bee health remains to be determined."

In 2005, a team of scientists led by the National Institute of Beekeeping in Bologna, Italy, found pollen obtained from seeds dressed with imidacloprid contains significant levels of the insecticide, and suggested the polluted pollen might cause honey bee colony death. Analysis of corn and sunflower crops originating from seeds dressed with imidacloprid suggested large amounts of the insecticide will be carried back to honey bee colonies. Sub lethal doses of imidacloprid in sucrose solution have also been documented to affect homing and foraging activity of honey bees. Imidacloprid in sucrose solution fed to bees in the laboratory impaired their communication for a few hours. Sub lethal doses of imidacloprid in laboratory and field experiment decreased flight activity and olfactory discrimination, and olfactory learning performance was impaired.

In 2010, Fipronil was blamed for the spread of colony collapse disorder among bees, in a study by the Minutes-Association for Technical Coordination Fund in France, which found that even at very low nonlethal doses, this pesticide still impairs the ability to locate the hive, resulting in large numbers of foragers lost with every pollen-finding expedition, though no mention was made regarding any of the other symptoms of CCD. Other studies, however, have shown no acute effect of Fipronil on honey bees. Fipronil is designed to eliminate insects similar to bees, such as yellow jackets (Vespula germanica) and many other colonial pests by a process of toxic baiting, whereby one insect returning to the hive spreads the pesticide among the brood.

In 2012, researchers announced findings that sub lethal exposure to imidacloprid rendered honey bees significantly more susceptible to infection by the fungus Nosema, thereby suggesting a potential link to CCD, given that Nosema is increasingly considered to contribute to CCD.

Also in 2012, researchers in Italy published findings that the pneumatic drilling machines that plant corn seeds coated with clothianidin and imidacloprid release large amounts of the pesticide into the air, causing significant mortality in foraging honey bees. According to the study, "Experimental results show that the environmental release of particles containing neonicotinoids can produce high exposure levels for bees, with lethal effects compatible with colony losses phenomena observed by beekeepers." Commonly used pesticides, such as the neonicotinoid imidacloprid reduce colony growth and new queen production in experimental exposure matched to field levels. They also reported they were able to replicate CCD with imidacloprid. Another neonicotinoid, thiamethoxam, causes navigational homing failure of foraging bees, with high mortality.

A 2012 *in situ* study provided strong evidence that exposure to sub-lethal levels of imidacloprid in high fructose corn syrup (HFCS) used to feed honey bees when forage is not available causes bees to exhibit symptoms consistent to CCD. The researchers suggested that "the observed delayed mortality in honey bees caused by imidacloprid in HFCS is a novel and plausible mechanism for CCD, and should be validated in future studies".

In March 2013, two studies were published showing that neonicotinoids affect bee long term and short term memory, suggesting a cause of action resulting in failure to return to the hive. Growth in the use of neonicotinoid pesticides has roughly tracked rising bee deaths.

Recent research is uncovering diverse sub-lethal effects of pesticides on bees. Insecticides and fungicides have been found to alter insect enzyme activity, their development, offspring sex ratios, mobility, navigation and immune function. Such findings are of great

14

concern given the large numbers and high levels of pesticides found in honey bee colonies.

Difficulty of evaluating the role of pesticides in CCD

It is difficult to evaluate pesticide contributions to CCD for several reasons. First, the variety of pesticides in use in the different areas reporting CCD makes it difficult to test for all possible pesticides simultaneously. Second, many commercial beekeeping operations are mobile, transporting hives over large geographic distances over the course of a season, potentially exposing the colonies to different pesticides at each location. Third, the bees themselves place pollen and honey into long-term storage, meaning that there may be a delay of anywhere from days to months before contaminated provisions are fed to the colony, making it virtually impossible to associate the appearance of symptoms with the actual time at which exposure to pesticides occurred.

Neonicotinoids are a new class of systemic, neurotoxic pesticides that are known to be particularly toxic to honey bees, which have rapidly taken over the global insecticide market since their introduction in the 1990s. These neonicotinoids, such as imidacloprid, clothianidin and thiametoxam, are used as seed treatments in hundreds of crops from corn to almonds, as well as in lawn care and flea products. The insecticides are routinely applied directly to the seed, and the developing plant absorbs them and expresses them in its pollen and nectar, thus causing a lethal problem for bees. Moreover, they persist in the soil for approximately 12 years, infecting any new plants that may be planted to replace them. These pesticides have been in use longer than we have known about CCD.

Italy, Germany, France and the European Union itself have taken action against neonicotinoids to protect their pollinators (and the European Union has already been sued by Syngenta and Bayer for this action), but in the United States, where science is mostly funded by the industries who benefit from the insecticides, only prophylactic labeling has been enacted by the EPA, while at the same time paradoxically approving new neonicotinoid insecticides for the market.   This is nothing new.   Around the same time, French beekeepers succeeded in banning neonicotinoids, the EPA under the Clinton administration permitted pesticides which were previously banned, including imidacloprid. In 2004, the Bush Administration reduced regulations further and pesticide applications increased.

Pesticides used on bee forage are far more likely to enter the colony through the pollen stores rather than nectar, due to the fact that pollen is carried externally on the bees, while nectar is carried internally, and, if too toxic, it could kill the bee before it gets back to the hive. Although not all potentially lethal chemicals, either natural or man-made, affect the adult bees, many primarily affect the brood. However, brood die-off does not appear to be happening in CCD. Most significantly, the brood are not fed honey, and adult bees consume relatively little pollen; accordingly, the pattern in CCD suggests that if contaminants or toxins from the environment are responsible, it is most likely to be through the honey, as it is the adults that are dying (or leaving), not the brood (though possible effects of contaminated pollen consumed by juveniles may only show after they have developed into adults).

To date, most of the evaluation of possible roles of pesticides in CCD have relied on the use of surveys submitted by beekeepers, but it seems likely that direct testing of samples from affected colonies will be needed, especially given the possible role of systemic insecticides such as the neonicotinoids such as imidacloprid, which are applied to the soil and taken up into the plant's tissues, including pollen and nectar, and which may be applied to a crop when the beekeeper is not present. The known effects of imidacloprid on insects, including honey bees, are consistent with the symptoms of CCD. For example, the effects of imidacloprid on termites include apparent failure of the immune system, and disorientation.

What can be done now

Some argue that, since the exact causes of CCD are still unknown, and that more due diligence should be conducted before taking action. However, certainly being proactive is a better idea. The practices that have been identified as possible causing factors are dangerous practices that should either be eliminated, reduced, or modified to have less of a negative impact on hives. As the commercial demand for pollination increases and the numbers of hives decline, stressors on the bees themselves are going to make this a very difficult proposition.

Long term solutions such as a sperm bank made of sperm from healthier bees, or the introduction of heartier sub species (such as those available from Russia) have been suggested. These are the types of potential solutions that require more research. Eliminating the use of pesticides, fungicides, and feeding with corn syrup are no-brainers.

For the latest information on methods of effective hive management and preservation techniques, visit: http://beeinformed.org/

CHAPTER 4: NATIVE BEES

We rely on honey bees to pollinate about three-quarters of the world's food. Most commercial farmers rent honeybee hives each year to provide pollination services. However, with the rapid destruction of honey bee hives by Colony Collapse Disorder, new ways of commercial pollination have been sought. The obvious ridiculous methods that have been proposed are human pollination (which is practiced in some parts of China where bee populations have been decimated) and tiny robotic bees. But the answer may be lying with the native bees that pollinated our plants before the arrival of the honey bee and apiculture. Many of these bees are endangered, but still with us.

Based on studies of cranberry farms in Wisconsin, the United States' largest cranberry producing state, cranberry farmers have been experiencing good yields without bringing in any honeybees at all. A study in New Jersey found similar results for watermelons. Strategies for attracting wild bees, who may be more efficient pollinators, include the avoidance of pesticides and herbicides, planting small patches of other flowering plants among crops, and planning crop rotations to ensure blossoms throughout the season can all encourage native-pollinator activity, as well as promoting diversity of the agricultural landscape by interspersing fields with uncultivated areas like grasslands and forests.

CHAPTER 5: THE BUMBLE BEE

The bumblebee is a native bee that is a member of the bee genus *Bombus*, in the family *Apidae*. There are over 250 known species, existing mainly in North America, but they are also in South America and Europe. They have been introduced to New Zealand and Australia as well.

Bumblebees are important pollinators of wildflowers, and also pollinate apples, kiwi, cashew, cotton, strawberries, brazil nuts, peppers, watermelon, tangerine, tangelo, persimmons, melons, cucumbers, squash, pumpkin, zucchini, loquat, sunflower, flax, lupine, apricot, cactus, sweet cherry, sour cherry, plum, almonds, peaches, nectarines, guava, pear, blackcurrant, red currant, rose hips, boysenberry, raspberry, blackberry, eggplant, naranjillo, rowanberry, clover, blueberry, cranberry, broad bean, vetch, cow pea and black-eyed pea, and they, along with solitary bees, are the only pollinators of tomatoes.

Bumblebees are social insects that are characterized by black and yellow body hairs, often in bands. However, some species have orange or red on their bodies, or may be entirely black. Like their relatives the honey bees, bumblebees feed on nectar and gather pollen to feed their young, but unlike honey bees, they don't store great amounts of honey.

The brightly colored pile of the bumblebee acts as insulation to keep the bee warm in cold weather. Bumblebees are typically found in higher latitudes and/or high altitudes, though exceptions exist. One reason for this is that bumblebees can regulate their body temperature, via solar radiation, internal mechanisms of "shivering" and radiative cooling from the abdomen.

Bumblebees form colonies, which are usually much less extensive than those of honey bees. This is due to a number of factors including the small physical size of the nest cavity, the responsibility of a single female for the initial construction and reproduction that happens within the nest, and the restriction of the colony to a single season in most species. Often, mature bumblebee nests will hold fewer than 50 individuals. Bumblebee nests may be found within tunnels in the ground made by other animals, or in tussock grass, as opposed to Carpenter Bees that burrow into wood. Bumblebees sometimes construct a wax canopy over the top of their nests for protection and insulation. Bumblebees do not often preserve their nests through the winter, though some tropical species live in their nests for several years. The queens can live up to one year, possibly longer in tropical species.

Bumblebees can visit flowers up to 1–2 kilometers from their colony. They also tend to visit the same patches of flowers every day, as long as they continue to find nectar and pollen, a habit known as pollinator or flower constancy. While foraging, bumblebees can reach ground speeds of up to 15 meters per second or 54 kilometers per hour.

When flying, a bee builds up an electrostatic charge, and as flowers are usually well grounded, pollen is attracted to the bee's pile when it lands. When a pollen-covered bee enters a flower, the charged pollen is preferentially attracted to the stigma because it is better grounded than the other parts of the flower. Pollen is removed from flowers deliberately or incidentally by bumblebees. Incidental removal occurs when bumblebees come in contact with the anthers of a flower while collecting nectar. The bumblebee's body hairs receive a dusting of pollen from the anthers, which is then groomed into its pollen basket. Bumblebees are also capable of buzz pollination, which consists of attaching to the flower and dislodging pollen with the vibrations from their wing muscles.

Once they have collected nectar and pollen, bumblebees return to the nest and deposit the harvested nectar and pollen into brood cells, or into wax cells for storage. Unlike honey bees, bumblebees only store a few days' worth of food and so are much more vulnerable to food shortages.

Queen and worker bumblebees can sting. Unlike a honey bee's stinger, a bumblebee's stinger lacks barbs, so it can sting repeatedly without injuring itself. Bumblebee species are not normally aggressive, but will sting in defense of their nest, or if harmed. They will generally ignore other animals and humans unless they are disturbed.

Bumblebees are increasingly cultured for agricultural use as pollinators because they can pollinate plant species that other pollinators cannot by buzz pollination. For example, bumblebee colonies are often placed in greenhouse tomato production, because buzz pollination releases tomato pollen more effectively.

Bumblebees are in danger of extinction in many developed countries due to habitat destruction and collateral pesticide damage. In Britain, until relatively recently, 19 species of native bumblebees were recognized along with six species of cuckoo bumblebees. Of these, three are extinct, eight are in serious decline, and only six remain widespread. Similar declines in bumblebees have been reported in Ireland, with four species being designated endangered, and another two species considered vulnerable to extinction.

A decline in bumblebee numbers could cause large-scale changes to the countryside, resulting from inadequate pollination of certain plants. The world's first bumblebee sanctuary was established at Vane Farm in the Loch Leven National Nature Reserve in Scotland in 2008.

Bumblebees native to North America are also vanishing, such as *Bombus terricola, Bombus affinis* and *Bombus occidentalis.* Another, *Bombus franklini,* may even be extinct. In 2011, the International Union for the Conservation of Nature set up the Bumblebee Specialist Group to review the threat status of all bumblebee species worldwide using the IUCN Red List criteria.

For more information on bumblebees and other pollinators and their preservation, you can contact the Xerces Society at http://www.xerces.org/ .

Pollinator Loss and Impacts on Plant Populations

Adding to the growing body of research on pollinator declines, another recent study shows that the decline of a single pollinator species significantly impairs plant reproduction. The study, entitled "Single pollinator species losses reduce floral fidelity and plant reproductive function," was published in the Proceedings of the National Academy of Sciences, out of the Rocky Mountain Biological Laboratory in Crested Butte, Colorado.

In the study, researchers examined 20 plots of meadows in the region, removing the most populous bumblebee species out of each plot, and patrolling them regularly to determine whether other pollinator species could fill the shortage for wildflower pollination. Instead, researchers found that in the absence of bumblebees, pollinator species foraged more widely, becoming less devoted to one flower species. Researchers specifically focused on the purple larkspur wildflower, and found that with broader foraging patterns, larkspurs were less likely to receive pollen from the same species, which is required for successful pollination. Because of changes to pollinator assemblages, larkspurs then produced 30 percent fewer seeds. These results demonstrate the wider consequences that loss of pollinators to pesticides can have on plant reproduction as well as ecosystem health.

CHAPTER 6: BATS, BIRDS AND OTHER POLLINATORS

Bats as Pollinators

Bats are very important pollinators in desert and tropical climates. The areas most dependent on bats for pollination are Africa, Asia, and the Pacific Islands.

Bats pollinate over 300 types of fruit in the world. This includes bananas, mangos, guavas and peaches and even the agave plant (which produces sweeteners and tequila). It is believed that over 500 different types of tropical plants are pollinated annually by bats.

Bats tend to like flowers that don't give off strong scents or offer bright colors. This is the opposite of what attracts bees. The types of flowers that the bats like also seem to have large quantities of nectar offered in them. Many experts believe that the birds and bees take the day shift and the bats and moths take the night shift in pollination.

Since bats fly longer distances than bees, and many are migratory in nature, they can carry the pollination process great distances, which helps diversify growth. Their movements are believed to continually introduce new plants to various locations.

Because bats are so important for pollination that is why they are protected in many areas. If the bats are eliminated in given locations it will severely hinder the development of many plants, fruits, and flowers. In addition bats are also well known for keeping harmful insects away from crops, such as June Beetles, Stink Bugs, and Corn Worm Moths. Without their help the use of harmful pesticides would significantly increase and be dangerous for humans.

Neonicotinoid pesticides are causing millions of bat deaths and are contributing to many other wildlife declines. Researchers conducted an in-depth review of existing literature and report these findings in the Journal of Environmental Immunology and Toxicology.

Birds as Pollinators

Hummingbirds, spiderhunters, sunbirds, honeycreepers and honeyeaters are the most common pollinator bird species. Plants that make use of pollination by birds commonly have bright red, orange or yellow flowers and very little scent. This is because birds have a keen sense of sight for color, but generally little or no sense of smell. Bird pollinated flowers produce copious amounts of nectar to attract and feed the birds that are performing the pollination, as well as having pollen that is usually large and sticky to cling to the feathers of the bird.

Hummingbirds are small birds which are found only in the Americas. Their ability to hover in mid- air by flapping their wings up to eighty times per second, plus their long curved beaks and a love for sweet nectar, makes them perfect pollinators. Hummingbirds burn up a tremendous amount of energy as they dart about from flower to flower and so they are attracted to the flowers that will give them something in return for their pollinating efforts, such as shrimp plants, verbenas, bee balm, honeysuckles, fuchsias, hibiscus and bromeliads.

Sunbirds and spiderhunters feed mainly on nectar, although, when feeding their young, they often also eat insects. Sunbird species can take nectar while hovering, but usually perch to feed. Their long curved beaks and brush-tipped tubular tongues make these birds particularly suited to feeding on and pollinating tubular flowers.

Honeyeaters resemble hummingbirds in many ways, but are not capable of lengthy hovering flight. Honeyeaters quickly fly from perch to perch, stretching or hanging upside down in order to reach the nectar with their highly developed brush-tipped tongue, while at the same time serving as a pollinator.

Birds are not known for pollinating food growing crops, but this does not mean that they are not important. If it were not for the assistance of our feathered friends, many plant species would be in danger of extinction.

Other Pollinators

Most people don't realize that, while bees are the most important pollinators, there are many other pollinators at work in the ecosphere, such as butterflies by day, moths by night, flies, such as syrphid flies, and even mosquitoes, which pollinate some types of orchids. The safety of these pollinators are compromised by the same threats the bees face in the current state of our environment.

CHAPTER 7: PESTICIDES

Pesticides have become an enduring feature of modern life, as they have been proven to increase yields in commercial agriculture. Insecticides have been very effective in controlling malaria, and have saved many lives. In 2007, the world used more than 5.2 billion pounds of weed killers, insecticides, and fungicides to do everything from protecting crops to warding off malaria. Worldwide pesticide use has been on a steady increase since then. But scientists have discovered that this widespread use of pesticides has also caused some serious problems. We cannot reasonably expect to introduce massive amounts of poison into the ecosphere without negative environmental effects.

Three long-term studies suggest that certain chemical pesticides can interfere with brain development in young children. Some experts suspect that a neonicotinoids are at least partly responsible for the recent collapse in bee populations. Australia's wheat farmers are facing one of the worst weed infestations in the world, caused in part by the overuse of herbicides, which led to herbicide resistant weeds. And an average of 300,000 people kill themselves each year by ingesting pesticides, largely in Asia, which accounts for one-third of the world's suicides. Researchers still don't understand the full impact of many chemicals on broader ecosystems and their full impact and unintended side effects on wildlife.

While other countries around the world are taking action to try to stop the bee apocalypse, such as the UK, which passed the Bees Act in 1980 and the European Union, which has banned bee killing pesticides, the United States has done nothing to halt the use of bee killing pesticides and is actually encouraging the continued use of genetically engineered plants and pesticides that have been proven in our courts and others around the world to be dangerous to bees and the environment.

Insecticides

The powerful lobby process of Dow Chemical is behind the Environmental Protection Agency's decision May 13, 2013 to approve a new neonicotinoid pesticide ingredient, *sulfoxator*, for use on crops, most of which depend on pollinators, without label warning protection. The approval comes as the EPA is in the midst of a study on the safety of neonicotinoids, which is not scheduled for completion for another four years. This is currently being challenged in the courts.

An appeal, filed in the 9th U.S. Circuit Court of Appeals July 10, by the National Pollinators Defense Fund, the American Honeybees Association, the National Honey Bee Advisory Board, the American Beekeeping Federation, and three professional beekeepers, seeks changes in the labeling of the poison, whose class has been proven to be fatal to honeybees and other pollinators and is the subject of a wide scale temporary ban in Europe that went into effect earlier this year. This may have resulted in a recent label change by the EPA, but it is not enough to solve the problem.

Neonicotinoid pesticides, such as Dow's *sulfoxator*, like its sister toxics, *acetamiprid, clothianidin* and *imidacloprid,* are some of the most widely used pesticides in the world, and have been responsible for rising bee deaths since 2005.

The EPA approved the use of the neonicotinoid *clothianidin*, co-developed by Bayer, in 2003 against the warnings of its own scientists. Despite EPA's findings that *clothianidin* poses a major risk to non-target insects, such as honey bees, and information from standard tests and field studies, as well as incident reports involving other neonicotinoid insecticides suggesting the potential for long term toxic risk to honey bees and other beneficial insects, Bayer's powerful lobby was able to get the toxic approved.

Studies have found residue of neonicotinoid pesticides in pollen and nectar, which has resulted in the elimination of entire colonies, as well as changes in the bees on a genetic level. The toxics remain in the biosphere for approximately 12 years, thus infecting new organic replacement plants. It is the equivalent of radiation poisoning for the pollinators, who continue to decline in massive numbers.

Fortunately, some action is being taken, but it needs tremendous grass roots support to overcome the powerful chemical lobby in Washington. Oregon Congressman Earl Blumenauer is proposing HR 2692, the "Save Our Pollinators Act", a bill to suspend the use of neonicotinoids, responsible for killing over 50,000 bumblebees last in 2013 in his state, which has reacted by a temporary ban on their use. The decimation of 37 million bees in Canada this spring is being attributed to neonicotinoid pesticides as well as genetically engineered corn, the use of which has been banned in Poland, where it has conclusively been proven deadly to bee colonies.

Four professional beekeepers and five environmental and consumer groups filed a lawsuit against the EPA March 21 in the Northern District Court of California, demanding that the regulatory agency suspend the use of pesticides *clothianidin* and *thiamethoxam*. The case, [*Ellis v. Bradbury, et. al.]*, No. 3:13-cv-01266-MMC, is in its early stages and should take a year or two to run its course.

The Environmental Protection Agency says its mission is to "protect human health and the environment." The time has come for the EPA to take a good hard look at what that mission really means, and to realize that it works for the public, and not the chemical companies.

The EPA did take a token step to address the problem in August 2013, when it unveiled its new label for neonicotinoid pesticides. Seen as a step in the right direction, it is more like putting a Band-Aid on a hemorrhage, however. Environmentalists argue that labels are not going to prevent the destruction of bee populations, favoring an all-out ban on neonicotinoids, such as the bans existing in Europe.

The new labels have a bee advisory box and an icon with information about routes of exposure and precautions that should be taken to reduce spray drift. The label says in red letters, "This product can kill bees and other insect pollinators." According to the EPA, these labels will prohibit the use of some neonicotinoid pesticide products where bees are present. The labels would be used for products containing *imidacloprid, dinotefuran, chlothianidin* and *thiamethoxam* — four of the most widely used neonicotinoids. Such chemicals kill insects with a nerve-poisoning effect.

The EPA said it would work with pesticide manufacturers to change their labels so that they meet federal standards. But critics say that this label will not prevent the most prevalent users of the pesticides, commercial farm operations, from using them, and they are probably right.

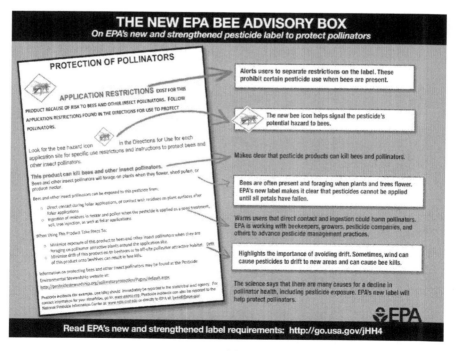

Factory farms make their money by producing a huge volume of product. That means everything about the planting, fertilizing, watering and harvesting needs to happen exactly on schedule. Therefore, the chances are slim to none that, on the day of a scheduled pesticide application, they will stop everything to determine which way the wind is blowing and if there are any bees around.

Rather than do its job, and remove these toxic chemicals from the shelves, the EPA is buckling under pressure from the pesticide industry. In the four years it takes to complete its "studies" on whether neonicotinoid pesticides should be banned, it continues to approve new neonicotinoid toxins for use in the ecosphere.

Features of Neonicotinoid Pesticides

• Persistent in soil and water soluble.

• Systemic pesticides applied at the root (as seed coating or drench) & then taken up through the plant's vascular system to be expressed in pollen, nectar & guttation droplets from which bees then forage and drink.

• Cannot be washed off.

• Nicotine-like, neurotoxic insecticides that bind to nicotinic acetylcholine receptors in insects' brains. (Bees are more susceptible to these insecticides because they have more of these receptors, as well as more learning and memory genes, and fewer genes for detoxification.)

• Widely used on more than 140 crop varieties, as well as on termites, flea treatments, lawns & gardens.

• Fastest-growing class of synthetic pesticides in history.

Strong correlations are found in the rise of neonicotinoid pesticides and Colony Collapse Disorder, as well as plummeting wildlife populations in areas where the chemicals are heavily used. Outbreaks of infectious diseases in many wildlife populations, including fish, amphibians, bats, and birds, coincide on a temporal and geographic scale with the emerging use of the pesticides. Non-target insects are also being wiped out, depriving wildlife of a food source.

These pesticides are so lethal because they are designed to disrupt the central nervous system. While very effective on pests, they are not specific to pests and appear to work on all animal life forms from invertebrates to mammals. In the case of honey bees, for example, the neurotoxins can kill them outright or cause "sub lethal" effects such as disrupting their ability to forage.

Researchers hypothesize that neonicotinoid pesticides have another sub lethal effect of damaging the immune system of a variety of wildlife, making them more susceptible to infectious disease outbreaks that correlate with use of the pesticide. This is thought to be a contributing factor in honey bees' inability to ward off the varroa mite that may a factor in Colony Collapse Disorder. Even after treatment for the mites, honey bees still cannot fight off the mites enough to prevent collapse.

Neonicotinoids persist in the environment, and do not break down quickly. These pesticides are typically applied to crop seeds. The chemical is ingested into the plant and travels to the growing shoots and flowers, where it is toxic to anything that eats any part of it. Honey bees take toxic pollen back to their hives in the pollen. The chemicals are also applied as a soil treatment. When it rains, the chemicals get washed into aquatic ecosystems.

Fungicide Exposure and Susceptibility to Disease

The newest USDA research adds to the growing body of evidence that shows pesticide exposure weakens honey bees' immune system making them more susceptible to parasites and pathogens. Researchers took pollen samples from crops that honey bees are known to pollinate including apples, watermelons, pumpkins, cucumbers, blueberries, and cranberries to determine exposure levels and Nosema infection.

In the study, researchers found 35 different pesticides in pollen, with samples containing, on average, nine different pesticides ranging in classes from oxadiazines, neonicotinoids, carbamates, cyclodienes, formamidines, organophosphates and pyrethroids. Of these, the report links eight pesticides as increasing the risk of Nosema gut parasite infestations. Researchers most frequently found fungicides in pollen samples, particularly chlorothanlonil, which is a broad spectrum fungicide used on apples and other crops. The presence of fungicides is of particular concern. Not only do fungicides increase risks of infection with deadly Nosema parasites, but they also generally do not carry warning labels to tell farmers to refrain from application while crops are blossoming and bees are foraging, that is, when bees are most susceptible to pesticide poisoning.

Honey bees that were fed pollen containing the fungicide chlorothalonil and collected at the hive entrance were almost three times more likely to become infected when exposed to the parasite Nosema, compared with control bees, which were not fed contaminated pollen.

The study shows that honey bees cannot sustain regular exposure to the vast array of agricultural chemical combinations that weaken honey bee immune systems and make them more susceptible to Nosema infestation. The difference between this new study and the majority of studies that had been done up to this point is that prior studies have examined honey bee exposure to only one chemical at a time.

Researchers also found that pesticides were evident in every pollen sample, even those that were collected from nearby wildflowers that were not sprayed. Co-author Dennis van Engelsdorp, PhD at the University of Maryland explained that, "It could be drift from when they sprayed their crop, but it also could be that the bees are picking it up and contaminating the pollen on the forage trip." He further stated that whatever the cause, we "need to better understand how pesticides are getting into the hive. Clearly it is not just from collecting pollen from the crops that bees are being used to pollinate."

In many cases, the pollen that bees brought back came primarily from plants other than the targeted crop. Some pollen samples contained very few pesticides, but the average number seen in a pollen sample was nine different pesticides, which could include insecticides, herbicides, miticides and fungicides.

Fungicides were the most frequently found chemical substances in the pollen samples. The most common was the fungicide chlorothalonil, which is widely used on apples and other crops. . The most common miticide found was fluvalinate, which beekeepers use to control varroa mites. However, the study concluded that treating varroa with miticides is akin to chemotherapy; it is bad for the bees; but not treating it is much worse for them.

"Our study highlights the need to closely look at fungicides and bee safety, as fungicides currently are considered safe and can be sprayed during the bloom on many crops," said van Engelsdorp.

The researchers only found neonicotinoids, which other studies have shown to be toxic to pollinators, in honey bees that were pollinating apples, suggesting the insecticide is just one part of a complex problem. This chemical-laden pollen was fed to healthy bees, which were then tested for their ability to resist infection with Nosema ceranae, a parasite of adult honey bees that has been linked to the overall problem of honey bee decline.

The most important finding, according to the researchers, is that bees fed pollen containing the fungicide chlorothonatil were nearly three times more likely to be infected by Nosema than bees that were not exposed to these chemicals, suggesting that ways of reducing bees' exposure to pesticides, and especially fungicides, should be instituted.

Herbicides

According to new research examining more than 300 studies, glyphosate, the active ingredient in Roundup®, is the most popular herbicide used worldwide. While most industry funded studies have concluded that glyphosate is not lethal to bees, it has been shown to be toxic to mammals. However, at least for some, the jury is still out. Naturalist Terrence Ingram claims that, in October 2011, Illinois officials seized or killed his glyphosate resistant bees, ruining 15 years of research, claiming they were conducting a foulbrood inspection. According to Ingram, not only were the bees not infected, but he also claims that the glyphosate in Roundup kills bees and the evidence of that was taken by the government killer inspector. Much more is known about glyphosate's impact on human health than its impact on bees, however.

Once called "safer than aspirin," glyphosate's reputation for safety isn't holding up to the scrutiny of independent research. More and more non-industry-funded scientists are finding links between the chemical and all kinds of problems, including cell death, birth defects, miscarriage, low sperm counts, DNA damage, and more recently, destruction of beneficial gut bacteria.

Monsanto (who is also the manufacturer of Agent Orange and DDT) asserts that glyphosate is minimally toxic to humans, but residues of it are found in all of the main foods of the Western diet, which consist primarily of sugar, corn, soy and wheat. Glyphosate's inhibition of cytochrome P450 (CYP) enzymes is an overlooked component of its toxicity to mammals. CYP enzymes play crucial roles in biology, one of which is to detoxify harmful xenobiotics introduced through the diet that are not naturally present in the body. Thus, glyphosate enhances the damaging effects of other food borne chemical residues and environmental toxins. Negative impact is insidious and manifests slowly over time as inflammation damages cellular systems throughout the body. Studies show that CYP enzymes acts synergistically with disruption of the biosynthesis of aromatic amino acids by gut bacteria, as well as the impairment of serum sulfate transport. Consequences are most of the diseases and conditions associated with a Western diet, which include gastrointestinal disorders, obesity, diabetes, heart disease, depression, autism, infertility, cancer and Alzheimer's disease.

Since chemical companies invented genetically engineered seeds designed to withstand heavy sprayings of glyphosate, global use of Roundup and related weed killers has jumped to nearly 900 million pounds annually. That is due to the fact that, since the crops are engineered to be resistant to Roundup, it can be sprayed on the entire field, not just on the weeds, making it much easier for farmers to manage weed kills. Glyphosate is a systemic chemical, meaning once sprayed, it travels up inside of the plants that people and animals eat and they consume the glyphosate as well as the nutrients in the plants. As more farm fields have converted to GMO crops, federal regulators have quietly allowed an increase in the levels of glyphosate allowed in your food, something from which we should see tragic long term consequences.

According to Stephanie Seneff, PhD, senior research scientist at Massachusetts Institute of Technology's Computer Science and Artificial Intelligence Laboratory, glyphosate acts as a potent bacteria-killer in the gut, wiping out delicate beneficial microflora that help protect us from disease. Harmful pathogens like Clostridium botulinum, Salmonella, and E. coli are able to survive glyphosate in the gut, but the "good bacteria" in your digestive tract, such as protective microorganisms, bacillus and lactobacillus, are killed off.

Even Monsanto knows about this. About 10 years ago, the company registered a patent for glyphosate's use as an antimicrobial agent. This damage to your digestive system can cause other problems, including "leaky gut," where the protective lining of the gut is compromised, allowing for toxins and bacteria to enter the bloodstream. This causes the body to send off an immune response to attack the wayward bacteria, potentially sparking autoimmune diseases.

Moreover, glyphosate can disrupt the gut's ability to create tryptophan, the building block of serotonin, an important neurotransmitter linked to happiness and well-being. Low serotonin levels have been linked to suicide, depression, obsessive-compulsive disorder, and other ailments. Not only does glyphosate hamper tryptophan production in your gut, it also lowers levels of it in plants, causing even more of a deficiency.

There are several things you can do, right now, to reduce your dangerous exposure to these chemicals, as well as contribute to saving the bees. They are:

• **Buy organic foods:** Roundup and other chemical pesticides and fertilizers are banned for use in organic agriculture. Instead, organic farmers focus on building healthy soil to support the growth of healthy plants. To find local sustainable farmers, try this site: http://Localharvest.org.

• **Avoid genetically engineered foods.** Avoid corn, which in the United States, is 90% GMO, and all corn products, including high fructose corn syrup (HFCS), which is present in most processed foods and drinks.

• **Avoid all processed foods.** The main glyphosate-laden foods that wind up in the food supply are corn, soy, and canola. Since these ingredients readily wind up in about 80 percent of processed foods, eating more whole foods (or choosing organic processed foods) can help lower your exposure to the chemical.

CHAPTER 8: THE CASE AGAINST GMO'S

According to the World Health Organization, Genetically Modified Organisms (GMOs) are "organisms in which the genetic material (DNA) has been altered in such a way that does not occur naturally." This technology is also referred to as "genetic engineering", "biotechnology" or "recombinant DNA technology" and consists of randomly inserting genetic fragments of DNA from one organism to another, usually from a different species. For example, an artificial combination of genes that includes a gene to produce the pesticide Cry1Ab protein (commonly known as Bt toxin), originally found in *Bacillus thuringiensis,* is forcibly inserted in to the DNA of corn randomly. Both the location of the transferred gene sequence in the corn DNA and the consequences of the insertion differ with each insertion. The plant cells that have taken up the inserted gene are then grown in a lab using tissue culture and/or nutrient medium that allows them to develop into plants that are used to grow GM food crops. This Bt toxin acts as an insecticide within the plant, killing insects that feed on it, and its lethal effect on bees is the reason that Monsanto's Mon810 GMO corn has been banned in Poland.

The Bt toxin, which essentially pokes "holes" in the cells of insects' stomachs, killing them, has been found to poke holes in human cells as well. In one study, it was found in the blood of 93% of pregnant women tested, and in the blood of 80% of their unborn fetuses, which gets into the brains of the fetuses, due to the fact that there is no blood-brain barrier at that stage of development.

Natural breeding processes have been safely utilized for the past several thousand years. In contrast, genetic engineering (GE) crop technology abrogates natural reproductive processes. Selection occurs at the single cell level, the procedure is highly mutagenic and routinely breeches genera barriers, and the technique has only been used commercially for 10 years. That is a very small time to evaluate the effects of contamination of these products on other plant life. The effects of natural breeding processes, on the other hand, can be seen over time. Genetic engineering is a new technology. Therefore, its long term effects on the organisms themselves, the ecosphere and the consumer are, as of yet, unknown.

The Supreme Court case of *Association for Molecular Technology v. Myriad Genetics,* 599 U.S. ____(2013), paved the way in the United States for the patenting of biological life forms. The biotech industry now seeks to control the world's food supply by disallowing farmer's use of saved seeds. Such use of GMO seeds would be a patent violation, subjecting the entire crop to the powerful remedy of seizure and destruction. In other words, once a commercial farm uses GMO seeds, they must buy all of their seeds from the industry, thus creating a world monopoly on food production.

Despite the differences between traditional breeding techniques and biotechnology, the biotech industry and the government, whose regulatory agencies are controlled by the industry, have concluded that GMO foods are "safe" based on the idea of "substantial equivalence," such that if a new food is found to be substantially equivalent in composition and nutritional characteristics to an existing food, it can be regarded as safe as the conventional food.

However, several animal studies indicate serious health risks associated with GMO food consumption including infertility, immune dysregulation, accelerated aging, dysregulation of genes associated with cholesterol synthesis, insulin regulation, cell signaling, and protein formation, and changes in the liver, kidney, spleen and gastrointestinal system. Moreover, despite their claim of safety, GMO manufacturers are spending millions of dollars to fight labeling efforts. They don't want you to know what you are eating.

Specificity of the association of GMO foods and specific disease processes is also supported. Multiple animal studies show significant immune dysregulation, including upregulation of cytokines associated with asthma, allergy, and inflammation. Animal studies also show altered structure and function of the liver, including altered lipid and carbohydrate metabolism as well as cellular changes that could lead to accelerated aging. Changes in the kidney, pancreas and spleen have also been documented. A recent 2008 study links GMO corn with infertility, showing a significant decrease in offspring over time and significantly lower litter weight in mice fed GMO corn. American pig farmers have reported infertility and false pregnancies in their livestock after feeding them GMO corn. The study also found that over 400 genes were found to be expressed differently in mice fed GMO corn. These are genes known to control protein synthesis and modification, cell signaling, cholesterol synthesis, and insulin regulation. Studies also show intestinal damage in animals fed GMO foods, including proliferative cell growth and disruption of the intestinal immune system.

Because of this mounting data, it is biologically plausible for genetically modified foods to cause adverse health effects in humans. In spite of this risk, the biotech industry claims that GMO foods can feed the world through production of higher crop yields. However, a recent report by the Union of Concerned Scientists reviewed 12 academic studies and indicates otherwise: "The several thousand field trials over the last 20 years for genes aimed at increasing operational or intrinsic yield (of crops) indicate a significant undertaking. Yet none of these field trials have resulted in increased yield in commercialized major food/feed crops, with the exception of Bt corn (a bee killer)." However, it was further stated that the increase in yields was largely due to traditional breeding improvements.

Therefore, because GMO foods pose a serious health risk in the areas of toxicology, allergy and immune function, reproductive health, and metabolic, physiologic and genetic health and are without any of their claimed benefits, the American Academy of Environmental Medicine (AAEM) believes that it is imperative to adopt the precautionary principle, which is one of the main regulatory tools of the European Union environmental and health policy and serves as a foundation for several international agreements. The most commonly used definition is from the 1992 Rio Declaration that states: "In order to protect the environment, the precautionary approach shall be widely applied by States according to their capabilities." Where there are threats of serious or irreversible damage, lack of full scientific certainty shall not be used as a reason for postponing cost-effective measures to prevent environmental degradation.

Another often used definition originated from an environmental meeting in the United States in 1998 stating: "When an activity raises threats to the environment or human health, precautionary measures should be taken, even if some cause and effect relationships are not fully established scientifically. In this context, the proponent of an activity, rather than the public, should bear the burden of proof (of the safety of the activity)." Do you hear that Monsanto? You have to prove your food is safe!

What does this mean to you? About 70% of the foods in your grocery store (in America) contain GMOs. Most products that contain soy (except most soy milk) corn, canola, and cottonseed oil will be GMOs unless they are 100% USDA certified organic. If you wish to avoid them, shop for organic foods, avoid processed foods, and buy local fresh vegetables and fruits or grow your own.

Monsanto, Dow, Bayer, DuPont and the other biotech giants have made genetically modified foods into a multi-billion dollar industry, making bold, unsupported claims that they will solve world malnutrition and increase crop yields. In reality, these genetically engineered seeds are made by the same companies who make pesticides and fertilizer, and who are now coming close to controlling the world's food supply, with the help of governments; especially the U.S. government. Here are some of their unsupported claims:

GMOs will not end world hunger

GMO crops have been conclusively proven to be irrelevant in the feeding of the worlds' hungry, according to a statement signed by 24 delegates from 18 African countries to the United Nations Food and Agricultural Organization. An I-Stat report, sponsored by the United Nations and the World Health Organization, authored by more than 400 scientists and signed on by 58 countries, concluded that genetically modified foods produce no greater yields and can have no possible contribution to end world hunger.

They do not produce greater yields, according to a comprehensive 2009 report by the Union of Concerned Scientists, which demonstrated that GMO soybean and corn produced no increase in intrinsic yield over conventional soybean and corn. And a 2008 study demonstrated that organic farming methods with little or no chemical fertilizer and pesticide use was able to increase crop yields by 116%. GMO crops are mostly engineered to contain their own pesticides or to be resistant to herbicides, or both. None of this translates to the end to world hunger and, even if they did produce higher yields, this would not impact world hunger at all, because the world already produces enough food to feed the world's population. World hunger is a socio-political and economic problem that GMOs will not solve. After all, they are not going to give them away, are they?

GMOs will not reduce pesticide use

Actually, GMOs are still treated with pesticides. The most popular GMO products are created by Monsanto called, "Roundup Ready" plants. These products are genetically engineered to not be killed by Roundup (glyphosate) so farmers can merely spray it on the plants, and it will kill all the weeds, but not the plants. Once sprayed on the plants, the Roundup enters the plants and is consumed by humans or animals who consume product, which causes the above-referenced long term health problems. Moreover, a 2012 study concluded that the rise of glyphosate-resistant "super weeds" has actually increased pesticide use in the last 15 years. The study estimated that if new strains of GMO corn and soybeans are approved for commercial use, herbicide use could increase by 50%.

GMOs are not safe to eat

The FDA does not test the safety of GMO crops. Instead, all GMO foods are assumed to be safe unless there is already evidence to the contrary. The FDA relies on self-reported data from the companies that manufacture the crops as to their safety. Moreover, due to legal and copyright restrictions surrounding GMO patents, independent scientists must ask for the chemical companies' permission before publishing research on their products. As a result, almost all of the long-term animal feeding studies that have ever been conducted on GMO feed have been carried out by the biotech companies themselves, with their own rules and using their own standards of reporting. What few independent studies have been conducted have shown a range of adverse health effects from reduced fertility to immune system dysfunction, liver failure, obesity and cancer.

As mentioned earlier, Roundup Ready crops are known to be laced with glyphosate, which causes the destruction of beneficial microfloral bacteria necessary to digestion, and results in conditions such as gastrointestinal disorders, obesity, diabetes, heart disease, depression, autism, infertility, cancer and Alzheimer's disease.

In a classic case of revolving door politics that the U.S. government is so famous for, the Obama administration's Deputy Commissioner of Foods, Michael Taylor, refuses to make FDA testing of GMO safety mandatory. Taylor worked for the FDA from 1976 to 1981, when he went into private practice at a law firm who represented Monsanto, only to return through the revolving door to the FDA in 1991. In 1988 he published an article entitled "The De Minimis Interpretation of the Delany Clause: Legal and Policy Rationale "in the Journal of the American College of Toxicology (now called the International Journal of Toxicology), which he had previously presented in December 1986 at a symposium on Topics in Risk Analysis, sponsored by International Life Sciences Institute Risk

Science Institute, Society for Risk Analysis, and Brookings Institution. The paper was delivered and published during the midst of a debate

and litigation over federal agencies' interpretation of the Delaney clause, a part of federal law written in 1958 that on its face, literally prohibits any chemical from being added, in any amount, to food that is processed, if that agent is carcinogenic.

As analytical instrumentation increased in power and more and more agents were found to be carcinogenic at very low levels, the agencies had developed a quantitative risk assessment approach to interpreting the Delaney Clause, which stated that if a carcinogen was present at levels less than 1 in 1,000,000 parts, the risk of that carcinogen was "de minimis" and it could be allowed on the market. In the article, Taylor presented arguments in favor of this approach. Advocates in favor of organic food have criticized Taylor for taking this stance and have attributed the stance not to a good faith effort to reasonably regulate, but to an alleged desire to benefit Monsanto financially.

Between 1994 and 1996 Taylor went back through the revolving door to the USDA, where he acted as Administrator of the Food Safety & Inspection Service. During that term he implemented a science-based approach to raising safety standards for meat and poultry production over the protests from industry, which has been called by food safety advocates "a truly heroic accomplishment (but that was the only one). Between 1996 and 2000, after briefly returning to King & Spalding, he then returned to Monsanto to become Vice President for Public Policy. In 2009, Taylor once again returned to government through the revolving door as Senior Advisor to the FDA Commissioner, and was appointed by President Obama on January 13, 2010 to another newly created post at the FDA, this time as Deputy Commissioner for Foods.

GMO technology is not the same as conventional breeding techniques

The industry argues that there is no difference between conventional breeding techniques and genetic engineering except for the time frame involved. What used to take years and years can now be accomplished in a laboratory in a short time, they say.

This is not true. Conventional breeding takes one strain of a certain crop, such as corn, and breeds it with another strain of that same crop. Genetic engineering takes genetic material from one species, such as a bacteria or an animal, and forces it into the genetic material of a crop, such as corn or cotton. This can be done by a variety of techniques, such as the use of gene guns to fire the genetic material into the cell of the target organism, a process that leads to random and unintended genetic mutations.

There is a need to label GMOs

The argument for why companies should not have to label GMOs is ridiculous. They simply think the public should not know what they are eating because it would "scare them." On the other hand, there are people who think that all foods should list what they are composed of, such as has been long required by law in food labeling.

There is an excellent short video by the Corbett Report exposing the myths of GMOs that can be found at: http://www.youtube.com/watch?v=ptDd9ftNaq8. But the best responses that have been made in response to the GMO arguments were made by 14 year old activist, Rachel Parent, who challenged a GMO proponent on his own show and destroyed him as well as all the arguments. You can see the video at: http://www.youtube.com/watch?v=HIXER_yZUBg

What types of foods are genetically modified?

You are probably eating many genetically modified foods. Almost all processed foods contain common ingredients like corn starch and soy protein, which are predominantly derived from genetically modified crops. In fact, GMOs are present in 60 to 70 percent of foods on US supermarket shelves, according to the Center for Food Safety. No meat, fish, and poultry products approved for direct human consumption are bioengineered at the present time, but most of the feed for livestock and fish is derived from GM corn, alfalfa, and other biotech grains. Only organic varieties of these animal products are guaranteed GMO-free feed. The following fresh fruits and vegetables are also genetically modified:

1. Papayas: In the 1990s, Hawaiian papaya trees were plagued by the ringspot virus which decimated nearly half the crop in the state. In 1998, scientists developed a transgenic fruit called Rainbow papaya, which is resistant to the virus. Now 77% of the papaya grown in Hawaii is genetically engineered, and there are bills currently being proposed in the state to abolish them altogether. GMO papaya has been banned in the European Union.

2. Milk: rGBH, or recombinant bovine growth hormone, is a GE variation on a naturally occurring hormone injected into dairy cows to increase milk production. It is banned for milk destined for human consumption in the European Union, Canada, Israel, New Zealand, and Australia. Many milk brands that are rGBH-free label their milk as such, but as much as 40 % of dairy products, including ice cream and cheese, contains the hormone.

3. Corn: While 90% of the corn grown in the United States is genetically modified, most of that crop is used for animal feed or ethanol and much of the rest ends up in processed foods. Sweet corn was GMO-free until last year when Monsanto rolled out its first harvest of sweet corn. Walmart has already begun to sell it without any labeling.

Monsanto is one of the largest and most notorious producers of many of the GMO foods that fill the produce sections of America's supermarkets. Bt corn, named after the *Bacillus thruringiensis* bacterium, is a form of sweet corn that has been genetically modified to include an insect-killing gene. This means the farmer doesn't have to spray with insecticide, because the insects die from eating the corn (but they spray it with herbicide anyway to kill the weeds). The same gene that attacks corn predators also appears to kill the Monarch butterfly and GMO corn has been banned in Europe for causing the death of bees. Moreover, all Bt corn planted in the U.S. is routinely treated with neonicotinoids.

4. Squash and zucchini: While the majority of squashes on the market are not GE, approximately 25,000 acres of crookneck, straightneck, and zucchinis have been bioengineered to be virus resistant.

5. Rice: While there are currently no varieties of FM rice approved for human consumption, a genetically modified variety of golden rice being developed in the Philippines has been altered to include beta carotene, a source of vitamin A. The argument in favor of this GMO product is to alleviate the deficiency of vitamin A in developing countries, but studies show that it would take a massive amount of daily consumption of this rice (over 27 bowls) to satisfy the minimum daily requirement of the nutrient.

6. Tomatoes: Tomatoes were the first GMO food to reach the market. Since I lived part time in the United States and part time in Europe, I always wondered why tomatoes in Europe tasted better, were different sizes, and rotted quickly and the ones in the United States had no taste. This is because the tomatoes in the U.S. are modified to be bigger, and to avoid rotting so quickly. Moreover, the original GMO tomatoes were resistant to antibiotics, which raises the concern that this may be passed on to humans.

7. Soy: Soy can be found in tofu, vegetarian products, soybean oil, soy flour, and numerous other products. Most strains of soy that make it to grocery stores have been genetically modified to resist herbicides. As Discovery.com points out, "Because soy is widely used in the production of other items (including cereal, baked products, chocolate and even ice cream), chances are everybody in the US is eating GM soy."

8. Others: Many vitamins may be sourced from GMO materials, and some bananas available in U.S. groceries stores have been identified as GMO. Some forms of alfalfa, used for animal feed, have been genetically modified. Vegetable oil is most likely from GMO soy, corn or canola. Likewise, margarine, is likely to by GMO as well, as it is made from vegetable oil. Many processed breads contain GMO additives. In addition, many breakfast cereals contain HFCS and soy products that are genetically engineered.

Beware of foods that are labeled as "natural" or made with "natural" ingredients. At the present time, there is no restriction for the use of this label with GMO foods, which is presently the issue of pending class action suits against General Mills, Campbell Soup Co., and the tortilla manufacturer Gruma Corp. Since the manufacturers and sellers of GMO foods are not required to label them in the United

States, you really cannot be sure of what you are eating unless it is certified organic. Organic foods cannot be grown with pesticides, antibiotics, or genetic modification.

Environmental Impact

The six largest producers of GE seeds- Monsanto, Syngenta, Dow Agrosciences, BASF, Bayer, and DuPont- are also the biggest producers of chemical pesticides. Monsanto's Roundup Ready crops are genetically engineered to be immune to herbicide so that farmers can destroy weeds without killing their crops. But the process has spawned Roundup resistant super weeds, leading farmers to apply greater and greater doses of the chemical or even resort to more toxic methods to battle back the super weeds. This amounts to hundreds of millions of extra pounds of pesticides being pumped into the ecosphere, which also translates into higher profits for the huge chemical companies.

A diet of grains and corn is far from a healthy diet. For proper nutrition, you also need to consume fresh fruits and vegetables. There is the attitude at some levels that the U.S. agriculture will shift almost entirely to crops like wheat, corn, and soybeans and that we will have to get our fresh produce from other countries. If this happens, the cost of fruits and vegetables to U.S. consumers will skyrocket.

This is unacceptable. But some people believe that the alternative of returning to classical agriculture and reducing the use of pesticides and eliminating systemic pesticides entirely is not economically feasible. And the powers that be are aligned with the corporate agricultural block that reaps the profits of pesticide intensive monoculture. To create a more bee friendly environment would require an environmentally friendly leadership attitude by elected officials with less preoccupation on short term profits and more thought given to long term consequences. This would require policy changes that favor environmentally friendly practices and discourage pesticide use.

Despite majority public support, most elected officials refuse to even support laws which would even require food labels to let consumers know which foods were GMO and which were treated with systemic pesticides. Congressmen and local elected officials from agricultural states are adamant in their support for the current use of pesticides and commercial agricultural practices. Besides the bee die-off, 'modern' agriculture has contaminated the drinking water in several states, and depleted the topsoil of natural nutrients and beneficial organisms. Remember that your health has been sold out the next time you go the voting booth and "unelect" any local or federal lawmaker you suspect has been bought by the "too big to fail" agriculture or chemical companies.

Contamination

A new study on genetically modified crops shows that they can spread their "benefits" to nearby weeds, making the weeds resistant to herbicides and defeating the purpose of their genetic modification. GMO crops are typically designed to resist glyphosate, the active ingredient in Monsanto's Roundup. This allows farmers to spray their crops so that the surrounding weeds die, but the genetically modified Roundup Ready crops (also produced by Monsanto) survive. The resulting super weed offspring is also resistant to Roundup.

It had previously thought that this wouldn't be a problem, because it was presumed that any genetic modifications would make wild plants less fit for their environment. Instead, researchers have found that the offspring of a weed and a GMO crop can actually give the weed advantages over other weeds. Weedy rice, a pest for many farmers, was shown to be Roundup resistant when mixed with GMO crops. Additionally, GMO-wild hybrids produced crops that photosynthesized more, and produced more shoots, flowers and seeds than wild plants, thus spreading the effects of contamination in the ecosphere and threatening to "choke out" existing species. Contamination will likely result in the domination of the GMO species and the extinction of contaminated species.

Recently in Oregon, a farmer discovered contaminated wheat that originated from Monsanto GMO trials years ago that were conducted many miles away. As a result, several countries have decided to cut their wheat imports from the United States. Wheat is the number one U.S. agricultural export.

Since GMOs are stronger than natural plants, and tend to overtake them, like weeds, it is likely that they will overtake and eliminate many beneficial plant species by the process of contamination, destroying plant biodiversity, a contributing factor to the decline in bee species. Moreover, GMOs' genes transfer from the genetically modified plants into the soil, contaminating it as well. Further, Roundup (glyphosate), which is routinely sprayed on hundreds of millions of acres of GMO Roundup Ready crops, destroys beneficial bacteria in the soil, promoting disease.

You are what you eat

Americans eat corn in snacks but also consume it in many products that contain high fructose corn syrup (HFCS). Proteins and fats in your food are incorporated into your body and brain with potentially profound effects on your health and even your behavior. A strand of hair can be tested to determine just how much corn is ingested by looking for a form of carbon found in corn. Americans' carbon is typically about 69% from corn.

Foods and condiments, such as ketchup, salad dressing, soda, cookies and chips all contain corn, usually in the form of high fructose corn syrup. This is translating to obesity and heart disease and potential for type 2 diabetes. Europeans eat a diet with far fewer processed foods and corn-based sweeteners. Americans also eat an extraordinary amount of soybean oil, another key ingredient in most processed foods. And, yes, both products are GMO.

CHAPTER 9: THE POWERFUL CHEMICAL LOBBY

Monsanto's corn is genetically engineered to produce a synthetic pesticide that has been proven to destroy bees and has been banned in Poland due to its bee-killing effects. Monsanto's GMO's are no longer welcome in Europe, and, as a result, the company no longer markets them there. Neonicotinoid pesticides, manufactured in the United States by Bayer and in Switzerland by Swiss GMO manufacturer and pesticide giant Syngenta, are being banned in Europe for massive bee deaths. Bayer and Syngenta have responded by suing the European Union. In the United States, due to the fact that giant companies like Monsanto can buy themselves legislation to immunize themselves from liability, don't expect the U.S. to ban the bee killing pesticides or plants anytime soon.

On March 31, 2013, the Senate passed the "Farmer Assurance Provision," which was signed into law by President Obama on March

26, 2013. The Provision has been dubbed the "Monsanto Protection Act," after the huge chemical conglomerate who makes the offending genetically engineered seeds.

The Plant Protection Act, passed in 2000 (7 USC section 7701 et. Seq.), authorizes the Dept. of Agriculture to prevent the introduction of "plant pests" into the United States food supply. Regulations classify genetically engineered plants as "plant pests." Persons wishing to plant such genetically engineered plants are prohibited from doing so unless granted non-regulated status by the Animal and Plant Inspection Service. In order to grant the non-regulated status, a detailed environmental impact statement must be prepared by the federal agencies responsible.

What the Monsanto Protection Act does is strip the federal courts of their power to protect the environment by making any court reversal of non-regulated status or a court injunction against growing plants that have been proven to be dangerous ineffectual, at the request of any grower or *seed producer,* who petitions the Dept. of Agriculture for an exemption. Hence the term "Monsanto Protection Act" as Monsanto is the largest producer of genetically engineered seeds in the world, and certainly footed the lobby bill for the provision. I believe that this provision is unconstitutional.

The bad news is that giant corporations throw giant money to lobbyists who control Congressmen and Senators who are supposed to work for you. The good news is that this provision is temporary and there is a huge grass roots movement calling for its repeal. So effective has been the movement, that Senator Jeff Merkley of Oregon (where non-approved Monsanto wheat recently contaminated wheat fields, nine years after and 500 miles away from Monsanto field trials), proposed an amendment to repeal the provision. Sadly (and not surprisingly) that amendment did not pass. Contamination of natural plant life by genetically engineered crops, which are engineered to resist insecticides and herbicides, occurs naturally by the process of pollination. The wheat crisis is being minimized by the government, despite the fact that it could affect wheat exports, which are mostly to countries who will not accept the genetically engineered wheat.

Even though the Monsanto Protection Act was a temporary measure, which was set to expire on September 30, 2013, the House of Representatives on September 10, 2013, extended it for three months in a short term spending bill. To make matters worse, Congressman Fred Upton of Michigan is also proposing a bill that would place GMO labeling under federal authority, taking that issue away from the states, where many labeling proposals are now being made.

You can be sure that the practice of bypassing courts by custom designed legislation will continue, which raises the question of the constitutionality of this practice. Courts must begin with the presumption that an Act of Congress is constitutional, unless the lack of constitutional authority is clearly demonstrated. *United States v. Harris,* 106 U.S. 629, 635 (1883). Does our constitution protect our environment from destruction and guarantee us the right not to be poisoned in our own backyard? "A law that impinges upon a fundamental right explicitly or implicitly secured by the Constitution is presumptively unconstitutional." *City of Mobile, Alabama v. Bolden,* 446 U.S. 55 (1979). Therefore, if the right to an environment free from destruction is a fundamental right, there is some authority to argue that the Monsanto Protection Act, and other laws that are sure to follow it, are unconstitutional.

The prevention of the destruction of our environment has been recognized internationally as a fundamental human right, and it is a violation of international law to subject individuals to scientific experimentation without their consent. "In 1955, the draft International Covenants on Human Rights was revised to add a second sentence to its prohibition of torture and cruel, inhuman or degrading treatment or punishment. The addition provided that "[i]n particular, no one shall be subjected without his free consent to medical or scientific experimentation involving risk, where such is not required by his state of physical or mental health." Annotations on the text of the draft International Covenants on Human Rights, at 31, U.N. GAOR, 10th Sess., Annexes, agenda item 28(II), U.N. Doc. A/2929 (July 1, 1955). The clause was later revised to offer the simpler and sweeping prohibition that "no one shall be subjected without his free consent to medical or scientific experimentation." ICCPR, supra, at art. 7. This prohibition became part of Article 7 of the ICCPR, which entered into force in 1976, and is legally binding on the more than 160 States-Parties that have ratified the convention without reservation to the provision. By its terms this prohibition is not limited to state actors; rather, it guarantees individuals the right to be free from nonconsensual medical experimentation by any entity—state actors, private actors, or state and private actors behaving in concert." See *Abdullahi v. Pfizer, Inc., 562 F.3d 163 (2nd Cir. 2009).*

The Ninth Circuit has upheld the prosecution of human rights violations in other countries under the Alien Torts Statute for actions which result in the destruction of the environment. *Sarei v. Tinto, PLC, 671 F. 3d 736 (9th Cir. 2011).* It stands to reason that the citizens of our own country should also have the same human rights.

Moreover, to allow the executive branch (such as the Dept. of Agriculture) to exempt persons affected by a court order or judgment from the effect of that order or judgment is a violation of the constitutional separation of powers. The separation of powers into the executive, legislative and judicial branches of government is fundamental to its survival and the preservation of liberty. These distinctions are designed to act as checks and balances against each other and the lines between them should not be blurred at the request of one individual or, in this case, one company, at the expense of the protection of our food supply and our very survival. "Our federal system provides a salutary check on governmental power. As Justice Harlan once explained, our ancestors "were suspicious of every form of all-powerful central authority." Harlan, *supra* n. 16, at 944. To curb this evil, they both allocated governmental power between state and national authorities, and divided the national power among three branches of government. *Unless we zealously protect these distinctions, we risk upsetting the balance of power that buttresses our basic liberties," Federal Energy Regulatory Commission v. Mississippi,* 456 U.S. 742 at 791 (1982), Justice O'Connor concurring and dissenting in part (*emphasis added*).

"The "concept of separation of powers," then, is exemplified by "the very structure of the Constitution. *Miller v. French,* 530 US 327, 341... "The Framers regarded the checks and balances that they had built into the tripartite Federal Government as a self-executing safeguard against the encroachment or aggrandizement of one branch at the expense of the other." *Buckley v. Valeo,* 424 U.S. 1, 122. "While the boundaries between the three branches are not `hermetically' sealed, *the Constitution prohibits one branch from encroaching on the central prerogatives of another." Miller,* 530 U.S. at 341,.

Accordingly, the Supreme Court has "not hesitated to strike down provisions of law that either accrete to a single Branch powers more appropriately diffused among separate Branches or that undermine the authority and independence of one or another coordinate Branch." *Mistretta v. United States* 488 U.S. 361, 382. (1989). . .In cases involving the Judicial Branch, the Court has traditionally acted to ensure "that the Judicial Branch neither be assigned nor allowed tasks that are more properly accomplished by other branches," and "*that no provision of law impermissibly threatens the institutional integrity of the Judicial Branch." Mistretta,* 488 U.S. at 383. "Even when a branch does not arrogate power to itself, the separation-of-powers doctrine requires that a branch not impair another in the performance of its constitutional duties." *Loving,* 517 U.S. at 757, *Mc Mellon v. United States,* 387 F. 3d 329 at 342 (4th Cir. 2004) (*emphasis added).*

Congress cannot vest review of the decisions of Article III courts in officials of the Executive Branch. *Hayburn's Case,* 2 Dall. 409 (1792), *Plaut v. Spendthrift Farm, Inc.,* 514 U.S. 211 (1995). Interference by the executive branch, with orders of the judicial branch violates the separation of powers. See *Clinton v. Jones,* 520 U.S. 681 (1997).

In this case, not only is the legislative branch interfering with the powers of Article III courts, but the interference also allows the executive branch (the USDA) to set aside and invalidate the enforcement of a court judgment, order or injunction. We must protect our courts from this interference. They are the only vestige of the government that we can actually reach out to as individuals and who must listen to and answer us. And they may be the only hope for the bees' (and our) survival.

CHAPTER 10: DESTRUCTION OF THE NATURAL HABITAT AND BIODIVERSITY

Habitat destruction is the process in which natural habitat is rendered functionally unable to support the species present. In this process, the organisms that previously used the site are displaced or destroyed, reducing biodiversity. Habitat destruction by human activity is principally for the purpose of harvesting natural resources for industry production, agriculture and urbanization. Habitat destruction is currently ranked as the primary cause of species extinction worldwide. It is a process of natural environmental change that may be caused by habitat fragmentation, geological processes, and climate change or by human activities such as the introduction of invasive species, ecosystem nutrient depletion, water pollution, air pollution, or noise pollution.

When a habitat is destroyed, the populations of plants and animals that occupied the particular habitat decline and extinction becomes more likely. Extinction may take place very long after the destruction of habitat, however, which is a phenomenon known as extinction debt. Habitat destruction can also decrease the range of certain organism populations. This can result in the reduction of genetic diversity and perhaps the production of infertile youths, as these organisms would have a higher possibility of mating with related organisms within their population, or different species. One of the best famous examples is China's Giant Panda, once found across the nation. Now it is only found in fragmented and isolated regions in the south-west of the country, as a result of widespread deforestation in the 20th Century.

Tropical rainforests have received most of the attention concerning the destruction of habitat. From the approximately 16 million square kilometers of tropical rainforest habitat that originally existed worldwide, less than 9 million square kilometers remain today. The current rate of deforestation is 160,000 square kilometers per year, which equates to a loss of approximately 1% of original forest habitat each year.

Other forest ecosystems have suffered as much or more destruction as tropical rainforests. Farming and logging have severely disturbed at least 94% of temperate broadleaf forests; many old growth forest stands have lost more than 98% of their previous area because of human activities. Tropical deciduous dry forests are easier to clear and burn and are more suitable for agriculture and cattle ranching than tropical rainforests; consequently, less than 0.1% of dry forests in Central America's Pacific Coast and less than 8% in Madagascar remain from their original extents.

Wetlands and marine areas have endured high levels of habitat destruction. More than 50% of wetlands in the U.S. have been destroyed in just the last 200 years. Between 60% and 70% of European wetlands have been completely destroyed. About 20% of marine coastal areas have been highly modified by humans. One-fifth of coral reefs have also been destroyed, and another fifth has been severely degraded by overfishing, pollution, and invasive species; 90% of the Philippines' coral reefs alone have been destroyed. Over 35% mangrove ecosystems worldwide have been destroyed. China, home to 10 percent of the wetlands in the world, have been destroyed during the process of urbanization. Since the 50's fifty percent of coastal wetlands have been destroyed. In the past forty years, 30% of wetlands have been decimated. Shrimp fishing has resulted in the destruction of many of China's Mangrove forests.

Habitat destruction vastly increases an area's vulnerability to natural disasters like flood and drought, crop failure, spread of disease, and water contamination. On the other hand, a healthy ecosystem with good management practices will reduce the chance of these events happening, or will at least mitigate adverse impacts.

Agricultural land can actually suffer from the destruction of the surrounding landscape. Over the past 50 years, the destruction of habitat surrounding agricultural land has degraded approximately 40% of agricultural land worldwide via erosion, salinization, compaction, nutrient depletion, pollution, and urbanization. Humans also lose direct uses of natural habitat when habitat is destroyed. Aesthetic uses such as bird watching, recreational uses such as hunting and fishing, and ecotourism usually rely upon virtually undisturbed habitat. Many people value the complexity of the natural world and are disturbed by the loss of natural habitats and animal or plant species worldwide.

Probably the most profound impact that habitat destruction has on people is the loss of many valuable ecosystem services. Habitat destruction has altered nitrogen, phosphorus, sulfur, and carbon cycles, which has increased the frequency and severity of acid rain, algal blooms, and fish kills in rivers and oceans and contributed tremendously to global climate change. One ecosystem service whose significance is becoming more realized is climate regulation. On a local scale, trees provide windbreaks and shade; on a regional scale, plant transpiration recycles rainwater and maintains constant annual rainfall; on a global scale, plants (especially trees from tropical rainforests) from around the world counter the accumulation of greenhouse gases in the atmosphere by sequestering carbon dioxide through photosynthesis. Other ecosystem services that are diminished or lost altogether as a result of habitat destruction include watershed management, nitrogen fixation, oxygen production, pollination, waste treatment; the breaking down and immobilization of toxic pollutants, and nutrient recycling of sewage or agricultural runoff.

The loss of trees from the tropical rainforests alone represents a substantial diminishing of the earth's ability to produce oxygen and use up carbon dioxide. These services are becoming even more important as increasing carbon dioxide levels is one of the main contributors to global climate change.

When biodiversity is lost, the environment loses many species that provide valuable and unique roles to the ecosystem. The environment and all its inhabitants rely on biodiversity to recover from extreme environmental conditions. When too much biodiversity is lost, a catastrophic event such as an earthquake, flood, or volcanic eruption could cause an ecosystem to crash, and humans would obviously suffer from that. Loss of biodiversity also means that humans are losing animals that could have served as biological control agents and plants that could potentially provide higher-yielding crop varieties, pharmaceutical drugs to cure existing or future diseases or cancer, and new resistant crop varieties for agricultural species susceptible to pesticide-resistant insects or virulent strains of fungi, viruses, and bacteria.

The rapid expansion of the global human population is increasing the world's food requirement substantially. Simple logic instructs that more people will require more food. In fact, as the world's population increases dramatically, agricultural output will need to increase by at least 50%, over the next 30 years. In the past, continually moving to new land and soils provided a boost in food production to appease the global food demand. That easy fix will no longer be available, however, as more than 98% of all land suitable for agriculture is already in use or degraded beyond repair.

Effect on Pollinators

Most of the world's plant species rely on animals to transfer their pollen to other plants. The undisputed queen of these animal pollinators is the bee, made up of about 30,000 species worldwide, whose flights aid in the reproduction of 90 percent of the world's flowering plants.

A UN sponsored report on honey bee and pollinator decline indicates a "sixth major extinction" of biological diversity is currently underway, caused by habitat destruction, pollution, pest invasion, and disease, leading to ecosystem havoc vital to human livelihood. The last major extinction occurred when the dinosaurs went extinct.

The United Nations Environment Program has released a study on a collapse of the world's honey bee colonies and presents scientific data and analysis regarding bee decline, including wild and controlled bee populations. The report, Global Honey Bee Colony Disorders and Other Threats to Insect Pollinators, includes authors who are world-leading honey bee experts, and issues an urgent warning over bee decline. Bees pollinate over 70 percent of the 100 crop species that provide 90 percent of global food supplies.

Colony decline is most prevalent in North America and has been observed in Europe since 1965. However, the report shows that since 1998, colony weakening and mortality has occurred particularly in France, Belgium, the UK, Germany, Switzerland, the Netherlands, Spain and Italy.

"The way humanity manages or mismanages its nature-based assets, including pollinators, will in part define our collective future in the 21st century," said Achim Steiner, UN Undersecretary-General and UNEP's Executive Director. "Human beings have fabricated the illusion that in the 21st century they have the technological prowess to be independent of nature. Bees underline the reality that we are more, not less, dependent on nature's services in a world of close to seven billion people," Steiner added.

Among the factors contributing to declines of honey bee populations is habitat deterioration and destruction. Human activities involving degradation, fragmentation and destruction of honey bees' natural habitat are considered as key causes of honey bee decline.

These activities lead to reduced food sources for honey bees and all pollinators. Turning large food habitat areas into smaller ones decreases food supplies for resident animals. Resulting population declines can no longer benefit plants. Wild pollinators need undisturbed habitat for nesting, roosting, foraging and sometimes specific larval host plants. As a result, they also suffer from habitat degradation and fragmentation.

Increased pathologies are another factor related to habitat deterioration. Various pathogens have been transferred from commercially-controlled bumblebee species used in greenhouse pollination programs, leading to a decline in some native bumblebee populations. Weak ecosystems can also increase development of parasites that impact controlled and wild pollinators.

Invasive species are introduced to pollinators when their natural habitats are destroyed. These include parasitic mites, such as the varroa mite, that feed on the bees' hemoglyph, spreading from hive to hive. The mites also introduce viral diseases and bacteria to the colonies and if left uncontrolled, will cause the premature death of the infected colonies.

Pollution is another factor leading to pollinator decline. Pollutants affect plants' abilities to produce chemicals that attract insects, in turn destroying vital scent trails. Scent trails that once traveled more than 2,000 feet in the 1800's now extend less than 600 feet from the plant, creating complications for pollinators as they search for food.

Climate change is also having an impact on pollinator declines. Shorter growing seasons, a fluctuation in new growth, flowering and aging periods all impact pollinator life cycles. Changing weather patterns, including droughts resulting from decreased rainfall lead to reduced plant vigor and delayed maturation of plants. Within the coming decades, a global loss of 20,000 flowering plant species is forecast by the International Union for Conservation of Nature (IUCN), according to the report.

Electromagnetic fields produced by electrically charged objects are also thought to influence bee behavior, as bees have small abdominal crystals containing lead, making them sensitive to these fields. One report calls for a more holistic approach to preserving and restoring all pollinator species, noting that pollination services require investment and good stewardship to preserve and sustain them. Habitat conservation can increase local pollinating species, which would be a benefit for nearby agricultural environments. Creating habitat designations for endangered plants should include considerations for wild pollinators.

Alternative farming methods, including the introduction of natural enemies of pests, insects and weeds is important for reducing wildlife exposure to toxic insecticides, fungicides and herbicides. The flowering season is a critical time for pollinators and any use of pesticide applications during that period should take that into consideration. Although controlled hives can be removed during such applications, wild populations of pollinators are completely vulnerable to such practices. Moreover, most of the popular pesticides are systemic, and persist in the soil for many years, contaminating new plant life.

The introduction of pollinator-friendly plants into the landscape increases feeding opportunities for pollinators and could enhance colonization, pollinator migrations and add strength to restoration programs.

Consideration of the different stages of pollinators' life cycles should be addressed as well. Pollinators require differing needs throughout their lives. For example, honey bee larvae require sufficient protein in the brood food during winter months to ensure their proper development. A sufficient amount of stored pollen in the colony in the autumn ensures chances for a successful adult population in the spring.

Food for thought

The impending global food crisis will be a major source of habitat destruction. Commercial farmers are going to become desperate to produce more food from the same amount of land, so they will use more fertilizers and less concern for the environment to meet the market demand. Others will seek out new land or will convert other land-uses to agriculture. Agricultural intensification will become widespread at the cost of the environment and its inhabitants. Species will be pushed out of their habitat either directly by habitat destruction or indirectly by fragmentation, degradation, or pollution. Any efforts to protect the world's remaining natural habitat and biodiversity will compete directly with humans' growing demand for natural resources, especially new agricultural lands.

A recent UCSB study that analyzed the USDA Census of Agriculture data from 1987-2007 concludes that the increase of agricultural production over the past four to five decades has corresponded to massive changes in land use often resulting in large scale monocultures separated by small fragments of natural land, and that these simplified landscapes should have more pest problems due to the lack of natural enemies and the increased size and connectivity of crops.

Governmental bodies at a local, national, and international scale should be urged to emphasize the following to minimize habitat destruction and loss of biodiversity:

1. Consider that the ecosystem services rendered by natural habitats are not replaceable.
2. Protect the remaining intact sections of natural habitat.
3. Educate the public about the importance of natural habitat and biodiversity.
4. Develop family planning programs in areas of rapid population growth and reduce expansion.

5. Find ways to increase agricultural output without increasing land for production and without damaging the ecosphere.

CHAPTER 11: CORPORATE GIANTS BUY OUT CONSERVATION MOVEMENT TO PRESERVE PROFITS

The foxes are guarding the hen house with the pesticide and GMO giant Monsanto sponsoring a "Bee Summit" and pesticide maker Bayer CropScience breaking ground on a new "Bee Care Center." This is just another example of big agribusiness taking over the conservation business. After all, they have the money, thanks to our purchases of their product as consumers. It should come as no surprise that the giants, who already control most of the scientific research on their own products, would want to control how their role in the extinction of the bees is perceived by the public. They want to be seen as the "good guys" while they continue to contribute to the problem.

Monsanto's Honey Bee Summit

Monsanto is an unlikely hero in the colony collapse disorder problem. Monsanto's Honey Bee Health Summit was held in mid-June 2013 at the company's headquarters in St. Louis, Missouri, in partnership with Project Apis M, a honey bee research organization, and the Honey Bee Advisory Council, a new organization made up of honey bee researchers and beekeepers. The multi-day summit was filled with talks on topics like nutrition and habitat loss, pesticides, varroa mites, and viruses. It was attended by commercial beekeepers, hobby beekeepers, and researchers among others.

"Hundreds of these types of meetings have gone on, but the one difference is that in the summit that we sponsored and Project Apis and the Honeybee Advisory Council hosted and led--the one difference is the ability to bring traditional agriculture to the table," says Maureen Mazurek, the stakeholder engagement lead at Monsanto. "We have agreed that focusing on solutions and creating bridges between the beekeeping community and the traditional agricultural community will make those possible solutions come to fruition."

In 2011, Monsanto bought Beeologics, a company that creates biological tools to address some of the pests and diseases that contribute to colony collapse. The company's first product, *Remembee*, prevents bees from developing something called Israeli Acute Paralysis Virus (IAPV).

Bayer's Bee Care Center

Bayer, another maker of neonicotinoid pesticides (and the co-inventor of them), claims to be committed to biodiversity, and has established "Bayer Bee Care Centers" to be part of its global "Bee Care Program". The European Bee Care Center opened in Monheim, Germany. While currently a Center in North Carolina is being developed. Bayer claims the centers will be a scientific and communication platform that consolidates Bayer's bee health projects. They claim they will also foster information sharing with external partners and promote new ideas to improve bee health. Never mind that Bayer has sued the European Union for banning neonicotinoid pesticides.

Big Ag's Unholy Alliance with Big Conservation

Big agribusiness has also, apparently, taken over big conservation, who have made "deals with the devils" in order to reach some kind of compromise at stopping the destruction of our environment.

Almost unnoticed, even by their own membership, the world's biggest wildlife conservation groups have agreed to a "live and let live" deal with big agribusiness. Led by the World Wide Fund for Nature (WWF), many of the biggest conservation nonprofit organizations including Conservation International and the Nature Conservancy have already agreed to a series of global bargains with international agribusiness. In exchange for vague promises of habitat protection, sustainability and social justice, these conservation groups are offering to "greenwash" industrial commodity agriculture.

The new conservation strategy arose from two basic realizations. The first was that agriculture and food production are the key drivers of almost every environmental concern. From issues as diverse as habitat destruction to the over-use of water, from climate change to ocean dead zones, agriculture and food production are globally the primary culprits. The second crucial realization for WWF was that forest destroyers typically are not peasants clearing land for farming, but national and international agribusinesses with bulldozers, responsible for the deforestation of thousands of acres at a time. Land clearance on this scale is an ecological disaster, but Claire Robinson of Earth Open Source points out it is also "incredibly socially destructive", as peasants are driven off their land and their communities are destroyed. According to the UN Permanent Forum on Indigenous Issues, 60 million people worldwide risk losing their land and means of subsistence from palm plantations.

By about 2004, WWF had come to realize the true impacts of industrial agriculture. Instead of informing their membership and initiating protests and boycotts, however, they embarked on a partnership strategy they call 'market transformation'.

Market Transformation

With WWF leading the way, big conservation has negotiated approval schemes for "Responsible" and "Sustainable" farmed commodity crops. The plan is to have agribusiness commit to reduce the 4-6 most serious negative impacts of each commodity crop by 70-

80%. If enough growers and suppliers sign up, then major rainforest areas can be saved.

There are market transformation schemes for palm oil, soybeans, sugar, biofuels, and for cotton, shrimp, cocoa and farmed salmon. These markets are each worth many billions of dollars annually and the intention is for these new "Responsible" and Sustainable" certified products to dominate them.

Producers and supermarkets will make advertising campaigns to buy "Responsible" and "Sustainable" products, which will be perceived by the public as approved safe for the environment. The goal of big conservation is that, if these schemes are successful, human rights, critical habitats, and global sustainability will receive a huge boost.

Reputational Risk

For big conservation these plans have a risk of guilt by association. The Round Table on Responsible Soy (RTRS) scheme is typical of these certification schemes. Membership in the schemes, which include signatures on press-releases and sometimes on labels, indicates approval for activities that are widely opposed. The RTRS, for example, certifies soybeans grown in large-scale chemical-intensive monocultures. They are usually GMOs, fed mainly to animals, and originate from countries with hungry populations. When 52% of Americans think GMOs are unsafe and 93% think GMOs should to be labeled, for example, this is a risk most organizations dependent on their reputations probably would not consider.

CHAPTER 12: HOW YOU CAN MAKE A DIFFERENCE

Now that you know how bad it is, you must be asking, "What can I possibly do to make a difference?" You should see by now that we can't count on our elected officials to do anything that cuts them off from their main corporate sources of campaign financing, so we have to do what we can as individuals to protect honeybees and natural pollinators like bumblebees, bats, butterflies and birds ourselves. Planting bee -friendly flowers for the pollinators and a vegetable garden for your family is a good solution for both our species. Encourage neighbors to plant non-treated seed, cut back or eliminate pesticide use, and use the 'organic' gardening method. If it is possible, establish a voluntary pesticide free zone in your neighborhood, beginning with your own home and encourage your neighbors to join. And, if you are a beekeeper, keep your hives at least two miles away from commercially grown corn and soybeans, and use "organic methods" of beekeeping. *How to Become an Amazing Beekeeper: Discover the Essential Steps for Beekeeping Like an Expert,* by David

Thomas, is an excellent guide on organic methods.

Too often we feel that we are at the mercy of our government or the collective will of society, and we think that there's nothing we can do as individuals to make a difference. But it's important to know that there are things you can do as an individual, even without even getting politically involved, that will make a difference in saving the bees. There are nine easy things you can do yourself right at home to make a difference. Collectively, if enough people do these things, we can go a long way toward saving the bees:

1. Plant bee-friendly flowers and herbs. But make sure first that they are not treated with neonicotinoid pesticides, because that will make the problem worse rather than better.
2. Bees like flowers on what we consider to be weeds, such as dandelions and clover. Let these types of "weeds" be present in your garden.
3. Don't use pesticides in your yard or garden.
4. Replace your lawn with bee friendly herbs and flowers. You will save water and help the bees at the same time.
5. Leave fresh water outside (in a container with gravel so as not to cause drowning) for a fresh water supply for bees.
6. Buy local and organic food. If enough of us do not support bee killing GMO's by not purchasing them, eventually they will stop making them.
7. Become more aware. Subscribe to news services or on Facebook or twitter to keep aware of the latest news on bees and their survival. A good source of news is: https://www.facebook.com/BeeBay.org
8. Make a seed bomb (recipe below) and "bomb" vacant lots and sparsely planted areas with bee-friendly flowers and herbs.
9. Keep a "bee-friendly" garden (see below).

Seed Bombs

Seed Bombs can be used to create a flower bed for bees in neglected areas. You can toss them over a fence in an empty lot and hope they grow to provide food and nourishment for humans or bees, depending on which seeds you decide to use, and turn your empty lots into a pollinator's oasis.

Clay Seed Bomb Recipe:

1. 5 Parts moist gray clay
2. 1 Part Compost
3. Seed of your choice

4. Add water and mold into 1 inch Balls. Set them aside to dry for at least 24 hours before you start tossing.

Have a bee-safe garden

How can you avoid bringing neonic-treated plants into a bee-safe garden? First, ask your garden center or nursery staff if their growers use neonicotinoid treated seed. Second, consider growing your own bedding plants and vegetables, especially those that attract bees and other pollinators, from seed. Several seed companies, such as www.terriotorialseed.com, www.kitchengardenseeds.com, and www.rareseeds.com state in their catalogs that they sell only untreated seeds. When buying seed from catalogs that do not specifically mention selling untreated seed, ask before ordering. Certified organic plants are pesticide-free and certified organic seeds are never treated with pesticides.

Next, begin saving your own seeds. Seed saving is a growing movement to preserve older or rare heirloom and native plants. But you don't need to grow rare plants to benefit from seed savings; you can easily preserve a lifetime supply of the seeds of your favorite plants. The only restriction to seed saving is that the seeds must come from open-pollinated (OP) plants. Unlike hybrid seeds (F1), OP seeds will reproduce true to the parent plant. Several websites, including http://www.seedsave.org provide information and instructions on seed saving. To find out what products to avoid in your garden, see: http://www.xerces.org/wp-content/uploads/2013/06/NeonicsInYourGarden.pdf

Growing your own fruits and vegetables

My mom has been growing her own vegetables and fruits for years. They are better tasting, for one thing, as well as healthier than their store-bought relatives. If you have any property at all, you can usually grow some kind of vegetables or fruits. If you are careful about where you get your seeds, should take all of the uncertainty out of whether you are providing your family with an uncontaminated food supply.

Bee friendly plants you can grow

The following are just some bee friendly plants that will help the bees, as well as enhance your vegetable and flower gardens:

Annuals	Perrennials	Fruits and Vegetables	Herbs
Asters	Buttercups	Blackberries	Bee Balm
Calliopsis	Clematis	Cantaloupe	Borage
Clover	Cosmos	Cucumbers	Basil
Marigolds	Crocuses	Gourds	Catnip
Poppies	Dahlias	Fruit Trees	Coriander
Sunflowers	Echinacea	Peppers	Cilantro
Zinnias	English Ivy	Pumpkin	Fennel
	Foxglove	Raspberries	Lavender
	Geraniums	Squash	Mint
	Germander	Watermelons	Rosemary
	Globe Thistle	Wild Garlic	Thyme
	Hollyhocks		
	Hyacinth		
	Rock Cress		
	Roses		
	Sedum		
	Snowdrops		
	Squills		
	Tansy		
	Yellow Hysopp		

Insect hotels

For those with a considerable amount of property, consider the construction of an insect hotel. An insect hotel is a structure created from natural materials, in a variety of shapes and sizes depending on the specific purpose or specific insect it is catered to. Most consist of several different sections that provide insects with nesting facilities, particularly during winter, offering shelter or refuge for many types of insects. Think of it as an on-land artificial coral reef.

Many insect hotels are used as nest sites by insects including solitary bees and wasps. These insects drag prey to the nest where an egg is deposited. Other insect hotels are specifically designed to allow the insects to hibernate, notable examples include ladybirds and butterflies. Insect hotels are also popular among gardeners and fruit and vegetable growers because they encourage insect pollination.

Materials to construct insect hotels with can include dry stone walls or old tiles. Drilling holes in the hotel materials also encourage insects to leave larvae to gestate. Therefore, a variety of different materials, such as stones and woods, are recommended for a wide range and diversity of insect life. Logs and bark, and bound reeds and bamboo are also often used. The various components or sizes of holes to use as entry of an insect hotel attract different species.

The best location for a hotel is a warm and sheltered place, such as a southern-facing (in the northern hemisphere) wall or hedge. The first insects are already active towards the end of winter and would be actively seeking for such a place to settle. Other species like to furnish their nests with clay, stone and sand, or in between bricks.

Even a simple bundle of bamboo or reeds, tied or put in an old tin can and hung in a warm place, is very suitable for solitary bees. The bamboo must be cut in a specific way to allow entry for the insects. Often people may add stems of elderberry, rose or blackberry shoots whose marrow can serve as a food source as well. There is a helpful video on how to build an insect hotel at:

http://www.youtube.com/watch?v=Zbn_wQYtaz8 .

CHAPTER 13: ACTING POLITICALLY

While our environment is being seriously threatened, it's selfish, corrupt, sleazy, dirty business as usual in Washington, and bees don't vote, so it's up to us to get the buzz out. We need to let our elected representatives, including the president, know that it is their responsibility to do what we want them to do and that we want them to save the bees. This is where most members of the public feel really helpless but, if you have access to a personal computer and an Internet connection, you can do your part to level the playing field and have a voice. After all, if the Internet can be used to topple a Middle East government, why not use it to tell your elected officials what you expect them to do, and impress upon them that you will vote for the "other guy" if they don't do it, the next time you find yourself at the polls.

There are sites where you can sign petitions to local, state, and federal governments, and you can even create your own petitions in a "user-friendly" environment and the petitions are delivered to your elected officials. Most of these sites will show you how to promote your cause with the use of the social networking phenomenon. Some of them will even send letters to elected officials at the touch of a mouse and prompt you to call them-even give you a script to use in your call.

In response to massive pollinator declines, recent legislation proposed by Representatives John Conyers (D-MI) and Earl Blumenauer (D- OR), H.R. 2692, *The Save America's Pollinators Act*, has called upon EPA to suspend the use of neonicotinoids, and to conduct a full review of scientific research before allowing the entry of other neonicotinoids into the market. You can find the supportive petition here and join the hundreds of thousands who are asking Congress to vote the way they want them to: http://www.credomobilize.com/petitions/tell-congress-stop-the-pesticide-that-is-killing-bees

Here are some other petitions circulating now to save the bees:

http://www.thepetitionsite.com/717/194/918/ban-bee-killing-pesticides/

http://www.thepetitionsite.com/203/680/260/repeal-the-farmer-assurance-provision-monsanto-protection-act-section-735-of-hr-933/

http://www.change.org/petitions/epa-save-our-bees-and-the-food-we-eat-ban-bayer-s-chemicals-now

http://www.avaaz.org/en/save_the_bees_global/

http://www.thepetitionsite.com/takeaction/673/611/950/

http://www.foe.co.uk/what_we_do/bee_cause_david_cameron_petition_39395.html

https://secure.38degrees.org.uk/page/s/ban-the-pesticides-that-are-harming-our-bees

http://action.fooddemocracynow.org/sign/save_the_bees/

More petitions can be found at this site: http://beepetitions.webs.com/

To get more involved in saving the bees, there are wonderful resources on Facebook that will provide you with useful information and events that you can participate in. Some of them are:

https://www.facebook.com/BeeBay.org?ref=hl

https://www.facebook.com/groups/wilsonvillebeesmemorial/

https://www.facebook.com/SaveBees

https://www.facebook.com/pages/Give-a-Shit-about-Bees/427686113928795

REFERENCES

Chapter 1

Berenbaum, Prof. May R. (29 March 2007). "Colony Collapse Disorder and Pollinator Decline

Chapter 2 and 3

http://en.wikipedia.org/wiki/Colony_collapse_disorder

Carter, Ecological Adaptation of Diverse Honey Bee (Apis mellifera) Populations, PLOS One 2010.

Status of Pollinators in North America, The National Academies Press 2013

"Research upsetting some notions about honey bees". ScienceDaily. December 29, 2006

Spivak M, Mader E, Vaughan M, et al., The plight of the bees, Environmental Science and Technology (45) 34-38, 2011.

Science Guide, Bees are Dropping Like Flies, http://www.scienceguide.nl/201308/bees-are-dropping-like-flies.aspx

Andrew C. Refkin (7 September 2007). "Virus Is Seen as Suspect in Death of Honeybees". The New York Times. Retrieved 2007-09-07.

JR Minkel (7 September 2007). "Mysterious Honeybee Disappearance Linked to Rare Virus". Science News (Scientific American). Retrieved 2007-09-07.

Amy Sahba (29 March 2007). "The mysterious deaths of the honeybees". CNN Money. Retrieved 2007-04-04.

"Multiple causes for colony collapse – report". 3 News NZ. May 3, 2013.

Robyn M. Underwood and Dennis van Engelsdorp."Colony Collapse Disorder: Have We Seen This Before?". The Pennsylvania State University, Department of Entomology. Retrieved 2010-05-02.

Benjamin Lester (7 March 2007). "Mystery of the dying bees". Cosmos Online.

Anonymous (1918). "Strange Behavior". American Bee Journal 58: 353. Retrieved 23 July 2012.

Oertel, E. (1965). "Many bee colonies dead of an unknown cause". American Bee Journal 105: 48–49.

Watanabe, M. (1994). "Pollination worries rise as honey bees decline". Science 265 (5176): 1170.Bibcode:1994Sci...265.1170W.doi:10.1126/science.265.5176.1170. PMID 17 787573.

"Wild bee decline 'catastrophic'". BBC News. 23 April 2008.

Johnson, Renée (7 January 2010). "Honey Bee Colony Collapse Disorder". Congressional Research Service. Retrieved 2012-05-24.

"Discussion of phenomenon of Colony disorder collapse". Canadian Honey Council. 27 January 2007. Archived from the original on 29 July 2007.

"A Survey of Honey Bee Colony Losses in the U.S., Fall 2007 to Spring 2008". Plos One. Retrieved 2012-05-24.

Van Engelsdorp, D., Underwood, R., Caron, D. Hayes, Jr., J. (2007) An Estimate of Managed Colony Losses in the Winter of 2006–2007: A Report Commissioned by the Apiary Inspectors of America. American Bee Journal.

, United States Department of Agriculture, Agricultural Research Service. Retrieved on 13 April 2012

"Why are Europe's bees dying?". BBC News. 20 November 2008.

Douglas, Ian (8 October 2010). "Study finds causes of Colony Collapse Disorder in bees". The Daily Telegraph(London).

Benjamin, Alison (2 May 2010). "Fears for crops as shock figures from America show scale of bee catastrophe". The Guardian (London).

Paul Mga, La mort des abeilles met la planète en danger, Les Echos, 20 August 2007 (French).

Alison Benjamin (2 May 2010). "Fears for crops as shock figures from America show scale of bee catastrophe | Environment | The Observer". London: Guardian. Retrieved 2010-06-22.

"Colony Collapse Disorder Action Plan" (PDF). USDA. 20 June 2007.

"CCD Steering Committee, "Colony Collapse Disorder Progress Report" (US Department of Agriculture, Washington, DC, 2009)" (PDF). Retrieved 2010-06-22.

Vanengelsdorp, D.; Evans, J.; Saegerman, C.; Mullin, C.; Haubruge, E.; Nguyen, B.; Frazier, M.; Frazier, J. et al. (2009). "Colony collapse disorder: a descriptive study".PLoS ONE 4 (8): e6481. Bibcode:2009PLoSO...4.6481V.doi:10.1371/journal.pone.0006481. PMC 2715894.PMID 19649264. |displayauthors= suggested (help)edit

http://www.sciencemag.org/content/336/6079/351.abstract

Kelland, Kate (29 March 2012). "Studies show how pesticides make bees lose their way". Reuters. Retrieved 2012-05-24.

European Food Safety Authority (2012) "Assessment of the scientific information from the Italian project 'APENET' investigating effects on honeybees of coated maize seeds with some neonicotinoids and fipronil" EFSA Journal10(6):2792

Damian Carrington (16 January 2013) "Insecticide 'unacceptable' danger to bees, report finds" The Guardian

"Honeybee problem nearing a 'critical point' | Environment | guardian.co.uk". London: Guardian. 13 January 2012. Retrieved 2012-05-24.

"High Levels of Miticides and Agrochemicals in North American Apiaries: Implications for Honey Bee Health". Plos One. Retrieved 2012-05-24.

Philipp Mimkes (2003-02). "Französische Regierung verlängert Teilverbot von Gaucho – Bienensterben jetzt auch in Deutschland" (in German). CGB Network.

Sven Preger (23 November 2003). "Verstummtes Summen – Französische Forscher: Insektizid ist Grund für Bienensterben" (in German). CGB Network.

"Betrayed and sold out – German bee monitoring – Walter Haefeker, Deutscher Berufs- und Erwerbsimkerbund". 12 August 2000. Retrieved 2007-04-26.

"Gaucho – ein Risiko, Studie: Mitschuld des Bayer-Pestizids für Bienensterben (Neues Deutschland)" (in German). 23 November 2003. Retrieved 2007-04-26.

"Imidaclopride utilisé en enrobage de semences (Gaucho®) et troubles des abeilles – Rapport final – 18 septembre 2003" (PDF) (in French). 18 September 2003. Archived from the original on 30 November 2006. Retrieved 2007-04-26.

"France: Governmental report claims BAYER's pesticide GAUCHO responsible for bee-deaths Coalition against Bayer-Dangers is calling for a ban". 2003-12. Retrieved 2007-04-26.

"Millions of bees dead – Bayer's Gaucho blamed". 26 November 2003. Retrieved 2007-04-26.

"Alarm Sounds on Bee-Killing Pesticides (by Julio Godoy)". 2004. Retrieved 2007-05-06.

Maria Mancilla, Les abeilles sont-elles en train de disparaître?, Rue 89, 29 August 2007 (French).

"EFSA Scientific Report (2006) 65, 1–110, Conclusion regarding the peer review of the pesticide risk assessment of the active substance fipronil" (PDF). 3 March 2006. Archived from the original on 16 June 2007. Retrieved 2007-04-26.

State notes small increase in pesticide use Western Farm Press

Pesticide Use Reporting California Department of Pesticide Regulation

Bonmatin JM, Marchand PA, Charvet R, Moineau I, Bengsch ER and Colin ME (29 June 2005). "Quantification of imidacloprid uptake in maize crops". J Agric Food Chem. 53(13): 5336–41. doi:10.1021/jf0479362. PMID 15969515.

Rortaisa A, Arnolda G, Halmbm M and Touffet-Briensb F. (2005). "Modes of honeybees exposure to systemic insecticides: estimated amounts of contaminated pollen and nectar consumed by different categories of bees".Apidologie 36 (1): 71–83. doi:10.1051/apido:2004071.

Bortolotti L, Monanari R, Marcelino J and Porrini P. (2003). "Effects of sub-lethal imidacloprid doses on the homing rate and foraging activity of honey bees". Bulletin of Insectology56 (1): 63–67.

Medrzycki P, Monntanari L, Bortolotti L, Sabatinin S and Maini S. "Effects of imidacloprid administered in sub-lethal doses on honey bee behaviour. Laboratory tests". Bulletin of Insectology 56 (1): 59–62.

Thompson H. (2003). "Behavior effects of pesticides in bees-their potential for use in risk assessment".Ecotoxicology 12 (1/4): 317–30.doi:10.1023/A:1022575315413.

"Scientists Untangle Multiple Causes of Bee Colony Disorder". Environment News Service. 2009. Retrieved 20 January 2011.

"Colony Collapse Disorder linked to Fipronil". Retrieved 2010-06-17.

"No acute mortalities in honey bee colonies (Apis mellifera) after the exposure to sunflower cultures". Retrieved 2010-06-27.

Sackmann, P; Rabinovich, M; Corley, JC (2001). "Successful removal of German yellow jackets (Hymenoptera: Vespidae) by toxic baiting". Journal of economic entomology 94 (4): 811–6. doi:10.1603/0022-0493-94.4.811. PMID 11561837.

Whitehorn, Penelope R.; O'Connor, Stephanie; Wackers, Felix L.; Goulson, Dave (29 March 2012). "Neonicotinoid Pesticide Reduces Bumble Bee Colony Growth and Queen Production". Sciencexpress. p. 1.doi:10.1126/science.1215025.

Lu, Chensheng et al (13 March 2012) In situ replication of honey bee colony collapse disorder Bulletin of Insectology 65 (1), 2012, ISSN 1721-8861, Accessed 7 April 2012

Henry, Mickaël; Beguin, Maxime; Requier, Fabrice; Rollin, Orianne; Odoux, Jean-François; Aupinel, Pierrick; Aptel, Jean; Tchamitchian, Sylvie et al. (29 March 2012). "A Common Pesticide Decreases Foraging Success and Survival in Honey Bees". Sciencexpress.
p. 1.doi:10.1126/science.1215039. |displayauthors=suggested (help)

"Pesticide tied to bee colony collapse | Harvard Gazette". News.harvard.edu. Retrieved 2012-05-24.

Chensheng Lu, Kenneth M. Warchol, & Richard A. Callahan (2012). "In situ replication of honey bee colony collapse disorder". Bulletin of Insectology 65 (1): 1–8.

Palmer, Mary J.; et al. (27 March 2013). "Cholinergic pesticides cause mushroom body neuronal inactivation in honeybees". Nature Communications 4: 1634.doi:10.1038/ncomms2648. Retrieved 31 March 2013.

Williamson, Sally M.; Geraldine A. Wright (7 February 2013). "Exposure to multiple cholinergic pesticides impairs olfactory learning and memory in honeybees". Journal of Experimental Biology 216 (10): 1799–807.doi:10.1242/jeb.083931. PMC 3641805.PMID 23393272. Retrieved 31 March 2013.

Dodd, Scott (30 March 2013). "Bees to EPA: Where's your sting?". Salon. Retrieved 31 March 2013.

Warner, Bernhard (19 February 2013). "To Revive Honey Bees, Europe Proposes a Pesticide Ban". BloombergBusinessWeek. Retrieved 6 March 2013.

Carrington, Damian (16 January 2013). "Insecticide 'unacceptable' danger to bees, report finds". The Guardian. Retrieved 9 March 2013.

Charlotte McDonald-Gibson (29 April 2013). "'Victory for bees' as European Union bans neonicotinoid pesticides blamed for destroying bee population". The Independent. Retrieved 1 May 2013.

Wozniacka, Gosia (21 March 2013). "Beekeepers sue EPA to ban pesticide, protect bees". Associate Press. Retrieved 22 August 2013.

Boyle, Alan (2 May 2013). "Pesticides aren't the biggest factor in honeybee die-off, EPA and USDA say". NBC News. Retrieved 22 August 2013.

"Blumenauer Announces Legislation to Protect Pollinators, Prevent Mass Bee Die-Offs".Blumenauer.house.gov. United States House of Representatives. Retrieved 27 August 2013.

Sheldon, Mary (3 August 2013). "Pesticides are not what bees need". Lexington Herald-Leader. Retrieved 22 August 2013.

Haugen, Stephanie (15 August 2013). "Hillsboro bee deaths still a mystery". Portland Leader. Retrieved 27 August 2013.

"Colony Collapse Disorder". Fruit Times (Pennsylvania State University) 26 (1). 23 January 2007.

a b "Bee Mites Suppress Bee Immunity, Open Door For Viruses And Bacteria".

Welsh, Jennifer (7 June 2012) Mites and Virus Team Up to Wipe Out Beehives Live Science, Retrieved 11 June 2012

Guzmán-Novoa, E., Eccles, L., Calvete, Y., Mcgowan, J., Kelly, P. G., and Correa-Benítez, A. (2009). Varroa destructoris the main culprit for the death and reduced populations of overwintered honey bee (Apis mellifera) colonies in Ontario, Canada. Apodologie. Published online 8 January 2010 atApidologie

Dr. Jamie Ellis (16 April 2007). "Colony Collapse Disorder (CCD) in Honey Bees". University of Florida.

Kim Kaplan (19 November 2007). "Imported Bees Not Source of Virus Associated with Colony Collapse Disorder". USDA. Retrieved 2007-11-29.

Cox-Foster, D. L.; Conlan, S.; Holmes, E. C.; Palacios, G.; Evans, J. D.; Moran, N. A.; Quan, P.-L.; Briese, T. et al. (2007). "A Metagenomic Survey of Microbes in Honey Bee Colony Collapse Disorder". Science 318 (5848): 283–287.Bibcode:2007Sci...318..283C.doi:10.1126/science.1146498. PMID 17823314.| displayauthors= suggested (help)

Genomic Study Yields Plausible Cause Of Colony Collapse Disorder at Science Daily on 2009-8-25

Johnson, R. M.; Evans, J. D.; Robinson, G. E.; Berenbaum, M. R. (2009). "Changes in transcript abundance relating to colony collapse disorder in honey bees (Apis mellifera)".Proceedings of the National Academy of Sciences 106 (35): 14790–5. Bibcode:2009PNAS..10614790J.doi:10.1073/pnas.0906970106. PMC 2736458. PMID 19706391.

Lev, D. (17 June 2013). "Israeli Scientist: Virus Causing Bees to Disappear". Arutz Sheva 7. Retrieved 23 June 2013.

Avraham, R. "Israeli Scientist Discovers Treatment to Save Bee Colonies". United with Israel. Retrieved 24 June 2013.

"Remebee". Beeologics. Retrieved 24 June 2013.

Higes, M; Martin, R; Meana, A (2006). "Nosema ceranae, a new microsporidian parasite in honeybees in Europe".Journal of Invertebrate Pathology 92 (2): 93–5.doi:10.1016/j.jip.2006.02.005. PMID 16574143.

Asian Parasite Killing Western Bees – Scientist, Planet Ark, SPAIN: 19 July 2007

Maria Mancilla, Les abeilles sont-elles en train de disparaître?, Rue 89, 29 August 2007 (French)

Dennis vanEngelsdorp, M.Frazier, and D. Caron (1 March 2007). "Tentative Recommendations for Hives Experiencing CCD" (PDF). Mid-Atlantic Apiculture Research and Extension Consortium.

Higes, Mariano; Martín-Hernández, Raquel; Garrido-Bailón, Encarna; González-Porto, Amelia V.; García-Palencia, Pilar; Meana, Aranzazu; Del Nozal, María J.; Mayo, R. et al. (2009). "Honeybee colony collapse due to Nosema ceranaein professional apiaries". Environmental Microbiology Reports 1 (2): 110–113. doi:10.1111/j.1758-2229.2009.00014.x. PMID 23765741.|displayauthors= suggested (help)

Cure For Honey Bee Colony Collapse? Science Daily article

Featherstone, D (2009). "Microbiology: Colony collapse cured?". Nature 458 (7241): 949.Bibcode:2009Natur.458T.949.. doi:10.1038/458949d.PMID 19396099.

Dr Wolfgang Ritter. "Nosema ceranae – Asian Nosema Disease Vector Confirmed—is this a new infestation or only now discovered?" (in translated into English). Albert Ludwigs University of Freiburg. Archived from the originalon 14 February 2007.

Sabin Russell (26 April 2007). "UCSF scientist tracks down suspect in honeybee deaths". San Francisco Chronicle.

"Scientists Identify Pathogens That May Be Causing Global Honeybee Deaths" (PDF) (Press release).Edgewood Chemical and Biological Center. 25 April 2007.

Jia-Rui Chong and Thomas H. Maugh II (26 April 2007)."Experts may have found what's bugging the bees". Los Angeles Times. Retrieved 2010-12-31.

Seth Borenstein (2 May 2007). "Honeybee Die-Off Threatens Food Supply, The Associated Press (5/2/2007)". Associated Press. Archived from the original on 5 May 2007. Retrieved 2007-05-07.

Paul Boring (25 April 2007). "Whidbey hives collapse".Whidbey News-Times.

Chapon, L., M.D. Ellis, and A.L. Szalanski. 2009. Nosemaand tracheal mites in the north central region – 2008 survey. Proceedings of the American Bee Research Conference. American Bee Journal 149: 585–586.

"Population genetics and distribution of "N. ceranae" in the United States, University of Arkansas Insect Genetics Lab". Comp.uark.edu. Retrieved 2010-06-22.

Szalanski, A.L., J. Whitaker, and P. Cappy. 2010. Molecular diagnostics of Nosema ceranae and N. apis from honey bees in New York. Proceedings of the American Bee Research Conference. American Bee Journal 150: 508

Leal, Walter S.; Bromenshenk, Jerry J.; Henderson, Colin B.; Wick, Charles H.; Stanford, Michael F.; Zulich, Alan W.; Jabbour, Rabih E.; Deshpande, Samir V. et al. (2010)."Iridovirus and Microsporidian Linked to Honey Bee Colony Decline". In Leal, Walter S. PLoS ONE 5 (10): e13181.doi:10.1371/journal.pone.0013181. PMC 2950847.PMID 20949138. |displayauthors= suggested (help)

Johnson, Kirk (6 October 2010). "Honeybee Killer Found by Army and Entomologists". The New York Times.

Drew Armstrong (7 October 2010). "Bee-Killing Disease May Be Combination Attack, Researchers Say". BusinessWeek. Retrieved 2010-11-21.

Kirk Johnson (6 October 2010). "Scientists and Soldiers Solve a Bee Mystery". The New York Times. Retrieved 2010-11-21.

Eban, Katherine (8 October 2010). "What a scientist didn't tell the NY Times on honeybee deaths". Money.cnn.com. Retrieved 2010-11-21.

Foster, Leonard (1 March 2011). "Interpretation of data underlying the link between CCD and an invertebrate iridescent virus". mcponline.org. Retrieved 2011-01-04.

Knudsen, Giselle; Chalkley, Robert (14 June 2011). "The Effect of Using an Inappropriate Protein Database for Proteomic Data Analysis". Public Library of Science. Retrieved 2011-06-14.

Hawthorne DJ, Dively GP (2011). "Killing Them with Kindness? In-Hive Medications May Inhibit Xenobiotic Efflux Transporters and Endanger Honey Bees". In Smagghe, Guy.PLoS ONE 6 (11): e26796.Bibcode:2011PLoSO...6E6796H.doi:10.1371/journal.pone.0026796.

Berenbaum, Prof. May R. (29 March 2007). "Colony Collapse Disorder and Pollinator Decline". Presentation to Subcommittee on Horticulture and Organic Agriculture, U.S. House of Representatives. The National Academies. Retrieved 2007-10-22., specifically, "Close to 100 crop species in the U.S. rely to some degree on pollination services provided by this one species—collectively, these crops make up approximately 1/3 of the U.S. diet [...] Although economists differ in calculating the exact dollar value of honey bee pollination to American agriculture, virtually all estimates are in the range of billions of dollars".

Alexi Barrionuevo (27 February 2007). "Honeybees, Gone With the Wind, Leave Crops and Keepers in Peril". New York Times.

Hannah Nordhaus (19 March 2007). "The Silence of the Bees". High Country News. Archived from the originalon 28 September 2007.

"Levels of polyandry and intracolonial genetic relationships in Apis koschevnikovi – International Bee Research Association". Ibra.org.uk. 21 April 2010. Retrieved 2012-05-24.

Sponsored by (3 December 2011). "Invasive species: Boom and bust". The Economist. Retrieved 2012-05-24.

Cooling, Meghan; Hartley, Stephen; Sim, Dalice A.; Lester, Philip J. "The widespread collapse of an invasive species: Argentine ants (Linepithema humile) in New Zealand".

Oldroyd BP (2007) What's killing American honey bees? PLoS Biol 5(6):e168. doi:10.1371/journal.pbio.0050168

Pickert, Kate (12 March 2009). "Postcard from Hughson". Time Magazine. Retrieved 12 December 2009.

Bee decline linked to falling biodiversity Richard Black, BBC News, 20 January 2010

Mao W, Schuler M A, Berenbaum M R (2013). "Honey constituents up-regulate detoxification and immunity genes in the western honey bee Apis mellifera". Proceedings of the National Academy of Sciences of the United States of America 110 (29 April 2013): 8842.doi:10.1073/pnas.1303884110.

Stever, H. J., Kuhn (2004). How Electromagnetic Exposure can influence Learning Process – Modelling Effects of Electromagnetic Exposure on Learning Processes.

Harst, W., Kuhn, J., Stever, H. (2006). "Can Electromagnetic Exposure Cause a Change in Behaviour? Studying Possible Non-Thermal Influences on Honey Bees – An Approach within the Framework of Educational Informatics". Acta Systemica 6 (1): 1–6.

Are mobile phones wiping out our bees? The Independent.

Eric Sylvers (22 April 2007). "Wireless: Case of the disappearing bees creates a buzz about cellphones".International Herald Tribune.

Chloe Johnson (22 April 2007). "Researchers: Often-cited study doesn't relate to bee colony collapse". Foster's Online.

Report on possible impact of communication tower on wildlife birds and bees Ministry of Environment and Forests, GOI 2011

Sainudeen Sahib, S. (2011). "Impact of mobile phone on the density of Honey Bees" (PDF). Mun. Ent. Zool. Vol. 6, No. 1.

"Zom-bees? Parasitic fly of bees different from fire-ant attacker". Uaex.edu. 13 January 2012. Retrieved 2012-05-24.

"A New Threat to Honey Bees, the Parasitic Phorid Fly Apocephalus borealis". Retrieved 2012-09-06.

"Parasitic fly spotted in honeybees, causes workers to abandon colonies". Retrieved 2012-09-06.

Duan JJ, Marvier M, Huesing J, Dively G, Huang ZY. 2008. A meta-analysis of effects of Bt crops on honey bees (Hymenoptera: Apidae). PLoS ONE 3:e1415

Peggy G. Lemaux: Genetically Engineered Plants and Foods: A Scientist's Analysis of the Issues (Part II). Annual Review of

Plant Biology Vol. 60: 511–559.

The Silence of Bees (2008)

"2009 documentary "Vanishing of the Bees"". Vanishingbees.co.uk – website explores possible causes of CCD. Retrieved 2010-06-22.

"What Are the Bees Telling Us? | The Story". Queen of the Sun. Retrieved 2012-05-24.

Pierre Terre Production, 2012, viewable on You Tube

"More than Honey – about the film". Retrieved 2013-07-28.

Spivak M, Mader E, Vaughan M, et al., The plight of the bees, Environmental Science and Technology (45) 34-38, 2011.

1Science Guide, Bees are Dropping Like Flies, http://www.scienceguide.nl/201308/bees-are-dropping-like-flies.aspx

Chapter 3

"Alternative Pollinators: Native Bees (Summary)". Attra.ncat.org. 12 October 2011. Retrieved 2012-05-24.

"Alternative Pollinators: Native Bees". Scribd.com. Retrieved 2012-05-24.

"Establishing a healthy population of native bees on your land". Conservationinformation.org. Retrieved 2010-06-22.

Madrigal, Alexis (5 June 2009). "Use of native bees to counter colony collapse disorder". Wired.com. Retrieved 2010-06-22.

Briton sends bee world abuzz with cure for killer bug. Dailyexpress.co.uk (25 August 2010). Retrieved on 2010-10-19.

Beekeeper Ron Hoskins breeds 'indestructible bees' in Swindon. Metro.co.uk (24 August 2010). Retrieved on 2010-10-19.

A+ for British Beekeeper as He Develops Mite-Resistant Strain of Honeybee. Fast Company (24 August 2010). Retrieved on 2010-10-19.

New Honeybee Breed Key to Combating Colony Collapse Disorder. TreeHugger. Retrieved on 2010-10-19.

National Bee Database to be set up to monitor colony collapse from Telegraph.com. Retrieved 10 March 2009.

Morse, R.A.; Calderone, N.W. (2000). "The value of honey ees as pollinators of US crops in 2000" (PDF). Cornell University.

Tepedino, Vincent J. (April 1981). "The Pollination Efficiency of the Squash Bee (Peponapis pruinosa) and the Honey Bee (Apis mellifera) on Summer Squash (Cucurbita pepo)". Journal of the Kansas Entomological Society 54 (2): 359–77. JSTOR 25084168.

Partap, Uma Partap and Tej. Pollination of apples in China. 2 September 2005

Partap, U.M.A., T.E.J. Partap and H.E. Yonghua (2001). "Pollination failure in apple crop and farmers management strategies in Hengduan Mountains, China". Acta Horticulturae (561): 225–230.

Chapter 5

http://en.wikipedia.org/wiki/Bumblebee

P. H. Williams (1998). "An annotated checklist of bumble bees with an analysis of patterns of description". Bulletin of the Natural History Museum (Entomology) 67: 79–152. Retrieved 30 May 2012.

P. H. Williams (2007). "The distribution of bumblebee colour patterns world-wide: possible significance for thermoregulation, crypsis, and warning mimicry".Biological Journal of the Linnean Society 92 (1): 97–118.doi:10.1111/j.1095-8312.2007.00878.x. Retrieved 9 July 2007.

"The Rusty-Patched Bumble Bee" Bio Web – Retrieved 13 February 2011.

Harder L.D. (1986). "Effects of nectar concentration and flower depth on flower handling efficiency of bumble bees".Oecologia 69 (2): 309–315. doi:10.1007/BF00377639.

"Map at: Bumblebees of the world". Natural History Museum. Retrieved 9 July 2007.

H. E. Milliron & D. R. Oliver (1966). "Bumblebees from northern Ellesmere Island, with observations on usurpation by Megabombus hyperboreus (Schönh.)". Canadian Entomologist 98 (2): 207–213. doi:10.4039/Ent98207-2.

B. Heinrich (1981). Insect Thermoregulation. Krieger Publishing Company. ISBN 0-471-05144-6.

Elaine Evans, Ian Burns & Marla Spivak (2007).Befriending Bumble Bees. St. Paul: University of Minnesota Press.

C. G. J. Van Honk, H. H. W. Velthuis, P.-F. Röseler & M. E. Malotaux (1980). "The mandibular glands of Bombus terrestris queens as a source of queen pheromones".Entomologia Experimentalis et Applicata 28 (2): 191–198.doi:10.1007/BF00287128.

D. J. C. Fletcher & K. Ross (1985). "Regulation of reproduction in eusocial Hymenoptera". Annual Reviews in Entomology 30: 319–343.doi:10.1146/annurev.en.30.010185.001535.

K. Walther-Hellwig & R. Frankl (2000). "Foraging distances of Bombus muscorum, Bombus lapidarius, and Bombus terrestris (Hymenoptera, Apidae)". Journal of Insect Behavior13 (2): 239–246. doi:10.1023/A:1007740315207.

W. E. Dramstad, G. L. A. Fry & M. J. Schaffer (2003). "Bumblebee foraging—is closer really better?". Agriculture, Ecosystems and Environment 95 (1): 349–357.doi:10.1016/S0167-8809(02)00043-9.

J. L. Osborne, S. J. Clark, R. J. Morris, I. H. Williams, J. R. Riley, A. D. Smith, D. R. Reynolds & A. S. Edwards (1999). "A landscape-scale study of bumble bee foraging range and constancy, using harmonic radar". Journal of Applied Ecology 36 (4): 519–533. doi:10.1046/j.1365-2664.1999.00428.x.

P. S. Blackawton; S. Airzee; A. Allen; S. Baker; A. Berrow; C. Blair; M. Churchill; J. Coles; R. F.-J. Cumming, L. Fraquelli, C. Hackford, A. Hinton Mellor, M. Hutchcroft, B. Ireland, D. Jewsbury, A. Littlejohns, G. M. Littlejohns, M. Lotto, J. McKeown, A. O'Toole, H. Richards, L. Robbins-Davey, S. Roblyn, H. Rodwell-Lynn, D. Schenck, J. Springer, A. Wishy, T. Rodwell-Lynn, D. Strudwick, and R. B. Lotto (2010)."Blackawton bees". Biology Letters 7 (2): 168–72.doi:10.1098/rsbl.2010.1056. PMC 3061190.PMID 21177694. Retrieved 5 January 2011.

Clarke, D.; Whitney, H.; Sutton, G.; Robert, D. (2013). "Detection and Learning of Floral Electric Fields by Bumblebees". Science 340 (6128): 66–9.doi:10.1126/science.1230883. PMID 23429701. Lay summary – Nature News & Comment (21 February 2013).

J. E. Maloof (2001). "The effects of a bumble bee nectar robber on plant reproductive success and pollinator behavior". American Journal of Botany (American Journal of Botany, Vol. 88, No. 11) 88 (11): 1960–1965.doi:10.2307/3558423. JSTOR 3558423.

Dave Goulson, Sadie A. Hawson & Jane C. Stout (1998). "Foraging bumblebees avoid flowers already visited by conspecifics or by other bumblebee

species". Animal Behaviour 55 (1): 199–
206. doi:10.1006/anbe.1997.0570.PMID 9480686.

Nehal Saleh, Alan G. Scott, Gareth P. Bryning & Lars Chittka (2007).
"Bumblebees use incidental footprints to generate adaptive behaviour at flowers
and nest". Arthropod Plant Interactions 1 (2): 119–127. doi:10.1007/s11829-007-
9011-6.

Nehal Saleh & Lars Chittka (2006). "The importance of experience in the
interpretation of conspecific chemical signals". Behavioral Ecology and
Sociobiology 61 (2): 215–220. doi:10.1007/s00265-006-0252-7.

Nehal Saleh, Kazuharu Ohashi, James D. Thomson & Lars Chittka (2006).
"Facultative use of repellent scent mark in foraging bumblebees: complex versus
simple flowers".Animal Behaviour 71 (4): 847–
854.doi:10.1016/j.anbehav.2005.06.014.

Livio Comba & Sarah Corbet. "Living larders for bumblebees". Natural History
Museum. Retrieved 20 June 2010.

B. O. Zimma, M. Ayasse, J. Tengo, F. Ibarra, C. Schulz & W. Francke (2003).
"Do social parasitic bumblebees use chemical weapons? (Hymenoptera,
Apidae)". Journal of Comparative Physiology A – Neuroethology Sensory Neural
and Behavioral Physiology 189 (10): 769–775.doi:10.1007/s00359-003-0451-
x. PMID 12955437.

R. M. Fisher & B. J. Sampson (1992). "Morphological specializations of the
bumble bee social parasite Psithyrus ashtoni (Cresson) (Hymenoptera,
Apidae)". Canadian Entomologist 124 (1): 69–77. doi:10.4039/Ent12469-1.

"Do bumblebees sting? Once or many times?". Straight Dope. Archived from the
original on 30 December 2007. Retrieved 9 July 2007.

"Bee Stings, BeeSpotter, University of Illinois". Beespotter.mste.illinois.edu. Retrieved 2012-05-25.

"On the Origin of Species By Means of Natural Selection, or, the Preservation of – Project Gutenberg". Gutenberg.org. 1 March 1998. Retrieved 2012-05-25.

"NRDC: OnEarth Magazine, Summer 2006 – The Vanishing". Retrieved 9 July 2007.

Inoue, Maki N.; Yokoyama, Jun; Washitani, Izumi (2007). "Displacement of Japanese native bumblebees by the recently introduced Bombus terrestris (L.) (Hymenoptera: Apidae)". Journal of Insect Conservation 12 (2): 135.doi:10.1007/s10841-007-9071-z.

Esterio, Gabriel; Cares-Suárez, Roxana; González-Browne, Catalina; Salinas, Patricia; Carvallo, Gastón; Medel, Rodrigo (2013). "Assessing the impact of the invasive buff-tailed bumblebee (Bombus terrestris) on the pollination of the native Chilean herb Mimulus luteus". Arthropod-Plant Interactions 7 (4): 467. doi:10.1007/s11829-013-9264-1.

Colla, Sheila R.; Otterstatter, Michael C.; Gegear, Robert J.; Thomson, James D. (2006). "Plight of the bumble bee: Pathogen spillover from commercial to wild populations".Biological Conservation 129 (4): 461.doi:10.1016/j.biocon.2005.11.013.

a b Graystock, Peter; Yates, Kathryn; Evison, Sophie E. F.; Darvill, Ben; Goulson, Dave; Hughes, William O. H. (2013). "The Trojan hives: Pollinator pathogens, imported and distributed in bumblebee colonies". In Osborne, Juliet.Journal of Applied Ecology. doi:10.1111/1365-2664.12134. Lay summary – BBC News (18 July 2013).

University of Newcastle-upon-Tyne (28 July 2006)."Scientists map the flight of the bumblebee". Science Daily.

Alan Harman (July 2003). "Bumblebee Shortage". Bee Culture 59.

P. H. Williams (1986). "Environmental change and the distributions of British bumble bees (Bombus Latr.)". Bee World 67: 50–61.

U. Fitzpatrick, T. E. Murray, A. Byrne, R. J. Paxton & M. J. F. Brown (2006). "Regional red list of Irish Bees" (PDF). Report to National Parks and Wildlife Service (Ireland) and Environment and Heritage Service (N. Ireland).

"World's first bumblebee sanctuary creates a buzz".Geographical 80 (10): 8. 2008.

"Bumble Bee Conservation". The Xerces Society for Invertebrate Conservation. Retrieved 20 June 2010.

"2011 Update" (PDF). =IUCN. Retrieved 7 October 2012.

John H. McMasters (March/April 1989). "The flight of the bumblebee and related myths of entomological engineering". American Scientist 77: 146–169.Bibcode:1989AmSci..77..164M. cited in Jay Ingram (2001). The Barmaid's Brain. Aurum Press. pp. 91–92.ISBN 1-85410-633-3.

Jay Ingram (2001). The Barmaid's Brain. Aurum Press. pp. 91–92. ISBN 1-85410-633-3.

50http://www.nature.com/scientificamerican/journal/v284/n6/pdf/scientificamerican0601-48.pdf

"Bumblebees Can't Fly". Snopes. Retrieved 9 April 2013.

"Bumblebees finally cleared for takeoff". Cornell Chronicle. 20 March 2000. Retrieved 26 January 2008.

John Maynard Smith. "Flight in Birds and Aeroplanes – Science Video". Retrieved 20 June 2010.

"Definition of Asynchronous muscle in the Entomologists' glossary". Department of Entomology, North Carolina State University. Retrieved 19 April 2013.

Brown, Lesley; Stevenson, Angus (2007). Shorter Oxford English dictionary on historical principles. Oxford [Oxfordshire]: Oxford University Press. p. 309. ISBN 0-19-923325-X.

"bumble-bee, n". Oxford English Dictionary. Oxford University Press. Retrieved 29 May 2011.

Chapter 7

http://www.realfarmacy.com/weapon-of-mass-wildlife-destruction-neonicotinoid-pesticides-at-the-root-of-global-wildlife-declines/#zolt7TI2zDQF08wd.99

Chapter 8

World Health Organization. (Internet).(2002). Foods derived from modern technology: 20 questions on genetically modified foods. Available from: http://www.who.int/foodsafety/publications/biotech/20questions/en/index.php

Smith, JM. Genetic Roulette. Fairfield: Yes Books.2007. p.10

Freese W, Schubert D. Safety testing and regulation of genetically engineered foods. Biotechnology and Genetic Engineering Reviews. Nov 2004. 21.

Society of Toxicology. The safety of genetically modified foods produced through biotechnology. Toxicol. Sci. 2003; 71:2-8.

Hill, AB. The environment and disease: association or causation? Proceeding of the Royal Society of Medicine 1965; 58:295-300.

Finamore A, Roselli M, Britti S, et al. Intestinal and peripheral immune response to MON 810 maize ingestion in weaning and old mice. J Agric. Food Chem. 2008; 56(23):11533-11539.

Malatesta M, Boraldi F, Annovi G, et al. A long-term study on female mice fed on a genetically modified soybean:effects on liver ageing. Histochem Cell Biol. 2008; 130:967-977.

Velimirov A, Binter C, Zentek J. Biological effects of transgenic maize NK603xMON810 fed in long term reproduction studies in mice. Report-Federal Ministry of Health, Family and Youth. 2008.

Ewen S, Pustzai A. Effects of diets containing genetically modified potatoes expressing Galanthus nivalis lectin on rat small intestine.Lancet. 354:1353-1354.

Kilic A, Aday M. A three generational study with genetically modified Bt corn in rats: biochemical and histopathological investigation. Food Chem. Toxicol. 2008; 46(3):1164-1170.

Kroghsbo S, Madsen C, Poulsen M, et al. Immunotoxicological studies of genetically modified rice expression PHA-E lectin or Bt toxin in Wistar rats. Toxicology. 2008; 245:24-34.

Gurain-Sherman,D. 2009. Failure to yield: evaluating the performance of genetically engineered crops. Cambridge (MA): Union of Concerned Scientists.

Lofstedt R. The precautionary principle: risk, regulation and politics. Merton College, Oxford. 2002.

Chapter 9

Executive Committee of the American Academy of Environmental Medicine on May 8, 2009, Submitted by Amy Dean, D.O. and Jennifer Armstrong, M.D.

Rayshell Clapper for redOrbit.com - Your Universe Online

Chapter 10

http://en.wikipedia.org/wiki/Habitat_destruction

Read more: http://digitaljournal.com/article/304525#ixzz2dfwYs4gR

Sahney, S. , Benton, M.J. & Falcon-Lang, H.J. (2010). "Rainforest collapse triggered Pennsylvanian tetrapod diversification in Euram eri ca" (PDF). Geology 38 (12): 1079–1082.doi:10.1130/G31182.1.

Pimm & Raven, 2000, pp. 843-845

Scholes & Biggs, 2004

Barbault & Sastrapradja, 1995

The Panda's Forest: Biodiversity Loss

"Tierras Bajas Deforestation, Bolivia". Newsroom. Photo taken from the International Space Station on April 16, 2001. NASA Earth Observatory. 2001-04-16. Retrieved 2008-08-11.

Barbault, R. and S. D. Sastrapradja. 1995. Generation, maintenance and loss of biodiversity. Global Biodiversity Assessment, Cambridge Univ. Press, Cambridge pp. 193–274.

Burke, L., Y. Kura, K. Kassem, C. Ravenga, M. Spalding, and D. McAllister. 2000. Pilot Assessment of Global Ecosystems: Coastal Ecosystems. World Resources Institute, Washington, D.C.

Cincotta, R.P., and R. Engelman. 2000. Nature's place: human population density and the future of biological diversity. Population Action International. Washington, D.C.

Geist H. J., Lambin E. E. (2002). "Proximate causes and underlying driving forces of tropical deforestation". BioScience 52 (2): 143–150.

Kauffman, J. B. and D. A. Pyke. 2001. Range ecology, global livestock influences. In S. A. Levin (ed.), Encyclopedia of Biodiversity 5: 33-52. Academic Press, San Diego, CA.

Laurance W. F. (1999). "Reflections on the tropical deforestation crisis". Biological Conservation91: 109–117.

McKee J. K., Sciulli P.W., Fooce C. D., Waite T. A. (2003). "Forecasting global biodiversity threats associated with human population growth". Biological Conservation 115: 161–164.

MEA. 2005. Ecosystems and Human Well-Being. Millennium Ecosystem Assessment. Island Press, Covelo, CA.

Primack, R. B. 2006. Essentials of Conservation Biology. 4th Ed. Habitat destruction, pages 177-188. Sinauer Associates, Sunderland, MA.

Pimm Stuart L., Raven Peter (2000). "Biodiversity: Extinction by numbers". Nature 403 (6772): 843–845. doi:10.1038/35002708. PMID 10706267.

Ravenga, C., J. Brunner, N. Henninger, K. Kassem, and R. Payne. 2000. Pilot Analysis of Global Ecosystems: Wetland Ecosystems. World Resources Institute, Washington, D.C.

Sahney S., Benton M.J., Falcon-Lang H.J. (2010). "Rainforest collapse triggered Pennsylvanian tetrapod diversification in Euramerica". Geology 38: 1079–1082. doi:10.1130/G31182.1.

Sanderson E. W., Jaiteh M., Levy M. A., Redford K. H., Wannebo A. V., Woolmer G. (2002). "The human footprint and the last of the wild". BioScience 52 (10): 891–904.

Scholes, R. J. and R. Biggs (eds.). 2004. Ecosystem services in Southern Africa: a regional assessment. The regional scale component of the Southern African Millennium Ecosystem Assessment. CSIR, Pretoria, South Africa.

Stein, B. A., L. S. Kutner, and J. S. Adams (eds.). 2000. Precious Heritage: The Status of Biodiversity in the United States. Oxford University Press, New York.

Temple S. A. (1986). "The problem of avian extinctions". Ornithology 3: 453–485.

Tibbetts John (2006). "Louisiana's Wetlands: A Lesson in Nature Appreciation". Environ Health Perspect 114 (1): A40–A43. PMC 1332684. PMID 16393646.

Tilman D., Fargione J., Wolff B., D'Antonio C., Dobson A., Howarth R., Schindler D., Schlesinger W. H., Simberloff D. et al. (2001). "Forecasting agriculturally driven global environmental change".Science 292: 281–284. doi:10.1126/science.1057544. PMID 11303102.

White, R. P., S. Murray, and M. Rohweder. 2000. Pilot Assessment of Global Ecosystems: Grassland Ecosystems. World Resources Institute, Washington, D. C.

WRI. 2003. World Resources 2002-2004: Decisions for the Earth: Balance, voice, and power. 328 pp. World Resources Institute, Washington, D.C.

IMAGE CREDITS

Cover : Monegasque Honey Bee, Copyright 2013 Valentina Eade

Inside Cover: Honey Bee, Copyright 2013 Valentina Eade

Table of Contents: Honey Bee, Copyright 2013 Valentina Eade

Figure 1: Albert Einstein, Licensed from Dreamstime

Figure 2: Russian Honey Bee, Copyright 2013 Valentina Eade

Figure 3: Russian Honey Bees, Copyright 2013 Valentina Eade

Figure 4: Russian Honey Bees, Copyright 2013 Valentina Eade

Figure 4: Native Bee, Copyright 2013 Valentina Eade

Figure 5: Bumble Bee, Copyright 2013 Valentina Eade

Figure 6: Bumble Bee, Copyright 2013 Valentina Eade

Figure 7: Hummingbird, Copyright 2013 Valentina Eade

Figure 8: Butterfly, Copyright 2013 Valentina Eade

SPECIAL THANKS

I wish to acknowledge the following people and organizations who were helpful in putting together and supporting this book:

My wife, Valentina, who conceived of the project to save the bees, and inspired me to write it.

My parents, Gordon and Joyce, who are always in my corner no matter what.

Give a Shit about Bees, https://www.facebook.com/pages/Give-a-Shit-about-Bees/427686113928795, for their support and promotion of the book.

Bee Against Monsanto, https://www.facebook.com/BeeAgainstMonsanto, for their support and promotion of the book.

The Principality of Monaco and SAS Prince Albert II, for their unrelenting advocacy for the world environment.

Made in the USA
Lexington, KY
18 February 2014